STUDY GUIDE

Joseph C. Hecht
Montclair State University

Ronald J. Ebert
Ricky W. Griffin

BUSINESS
ESSENTIALS

SECOND EDITION

Prentice Hall, Upper Saddle River, NJ 07458

Acquisitions editor: Donald J. Hull
Assistant editor: John Larkin
Project editor: Mark Andreotti
Manufacturing buyer: Arnold Vila

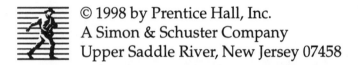

© 1998 by Prentice Hall, Inc.
A Simon & Schuster Company
Upper Saddle River, New Jersey 07458

Printed in the United States of America

10   9   8   7   6   5   4   3   2

ISBN 0-13-782822-5

Prentice-Hall International (UK) Limited, *London*
Prentice-Hall of Australia Pty. Limited, *Sydney*
Prentice-Hall Canada Inc., *Toronto*
Prentice-Hall Hispanoamericana, S.A., *Mexico*
Prentice-Hall of India Private Limited, *New Delhi*
Prentice-Hall of Japan, Inc., *Tokyo*
Simon & Schuster Asia Pte. Ltd., *Singapore*
Editora Prentice-Hall do Brasil, Ltda., *Rio de Janeiro*

TABLE OF CONTENTS

CHAPTER 1
UNDERSTANDING THE U.S. BUSINESS SYSTEM

CHAPTER OVERVIEW

Although economic systems around the world differ (Capitalism vs. Communism and Socialism) the basic obligation of each system is to allocate resources to its citizens. Economic systems differ according to ownership of its resources, often called factors of production. Labor, Capital, Natural Resources and Entrepreneurship play a major part in production. In capitalistic systems ownership of the factors of production is private and not owned by the government. In Communistic and Socialistic countries the government owns and operates most sources of production. In the United States known for its Market Economy supply and demand plays an important part in production. Competition plays an important part in the supply and demand scene. There are four types of competition: a.) Pure competition where no single firm is powerful enough to influence the price of its product or service in the market place. b.) Monopolistic competition where there are fewer sellers than in pure competition and c.) Oligopoly exists when sellers are very large in size and competition cannot usually build to compete with the giants. d. Monopoly exits when an industry has only one producer. Nearly every economic system has three broad goals: stability, full employment and growth. To judge the success of an economic system in meeting its goal, economists use one or more of four measures: gross national and gross domestic product, productivity, balance of trade and national debt.

CHAPTER OBJECTIVES

1. Describe different types of economic systems according to the means by which they control the factors of production.

2. Show how supply and demand affect resource distribution in the United States.

3. Identify the elements of private enterprise and explain how private enterprise differs from a controlled economy.

4. Explain the criteria for evaluating the success of an economic system in meeting its goals and show how the federal government attempts to manage the U.S. economy.

5. Describe how the difference of a positive and a negative balance of trade affects a country.

6. Describe the basic issues in creating a corporation.

OPENING VIGNETTE: TIRED OF MICKEY MOUSE VACATIONS?

The oldest of the 76 million Baby Boomer generation reached the age of 50 in 1996. They are no longer interested in Walt Disney World as a vacation spot. These empty nesters are too big a potential market for Disney to neglect. With an investment of many millions of dollars and an understanding that this will have to be a long term investment, a new idea was born: The Walt Disney Institute. This 75 acre resort-within-a-resort will have bird watching, cartoon animation, rock climbing, gourmet cooking, spiritual inquiry and more. Market research revealed this type of vacation was particularly attractive to baby boomers who had the money to spend and were willing to spend it on vacations.

Disney decided on shorter vacations for this group. These vacations will be balanced between education and entertainment at special introductory rates for the first 100 days. The Institute will be advertised by traditional means and depend heavily on word-of-mouth. The Institute is expected to attract 100,000 visitors a year. The program will eventually be used on future TV and direct-to-video programming.

Their decision came after a thorough marketing research program that the "boomer" demographics fit a Disney vacation plan. The Disney organization thus completed the plan.

After reading this vignette the reader should gain an insight into American business's everlasting search for new horizons. They want to plan a "product" to fit the demographics of a potential customer and to understand that it may take a long time to get a profitable return on the investments. Without the benefit of market research to uncover what a particular group wants, it would be very difficult to plan, build and expect a group to utilize the facilities.

KEY TERMS

Business - An organization that provides goods or services in order to earn profits.

Profits - The difference between a business's revenues and its expenses.

Economic system - A nation's system for allocating its resources among its citizens.

Factors of production - Resources used in the production of goods and services -- natural resources, labor, capital, and entrepreneurs.

Labor (or **Human Resources**) - The physical and mental capabilities of people as they contribute to economic production.

Capital - The funds needed to create and operate a business enterprise.

Natural resources - Materials supplied by nature -- for example, land, water, mineral deposits, and trees.

Planned economy - Economy that relies on a centralized government to control all or most of the factors of production and allocation decisions.

Market economy - Economy in which individuals control production and allocation decisions through supply and demand.

Market - Mechanisms for exchange between buyers and sellers of a particular good or service.

Capitalism - Market economy that provides for private ownership of production and encourages entrepreneurship by offering profits as an incentive.

Mixed market economy - Economic system featuring characteristics of both planned and market economies.

Privatization - Process of converting government enterprises into privately owned companies.

Socialism - Planned economic system in which the government owns and operates only selected major sources of production.

Demand - The willingness and ability of buyers to purchase a good or service.

Supply - The willingness and ability of producers to offer a good or service for sale.

Law of demand - Principle that buyers will purchase (demand) more of a product as its price drops and less as its price increases.

Law of supply - Principle that producers will offer (supply) more of a product for sale as its price rises and less as its price drops.

Demand and supply schedule - Assessment of the relationships between different levels of demand and supply at different price levels.

Demand curve - Graph showing how many units of a product will be demanded (bought) at different prices.

Supply curve - Graph showing how many units of a product will be supplied (offered for sale) at different prices.

Market price (or Equilibrium price) - Profit-maximizing price at which the quantity of goods demanded and the quantity of goods supplied are equal.

Surplus - Situation in which quantity supplied exceeds quantity demanded.

Shortage - Situation in which quantity demanded exceeds quantity supplied.

Private enterprise - Economic system that allows individuals to pursue their own interests without undue governmental restriction.

Private property rights - The right to buy, own, use, and sell almost any form of property.

Competition - Vying among businesses for the same resources or customers.

Pure competition - Market or industry characterized by a large number of small firms producing an identical product.

Monopolistic competition -Market or industry characterized by a large number of buyers and a relatively large number of sellers trying to differentiate their products from those of competitors.

Oligopoly - Market or industry characterized by a handful of (generally large) sellers with the power to influence the prices of their products.

Monopoly - Market or industry in which there is only one producer, which can therefore set the price of its products.

Natural monopoly - Industry in which one company can most efficiently supply all needed goods or services.

Stability - Condition on which the balance between the money available in an economy and the goods produced in it are growing at about the same rate.

Inflation - Phenomenon of widespread price increases throughout an economic system.

Recession - period characterized by decreases in employment, income, and production.

Depression - Particularly severe and long-lasting recession

Unemployment - Level of joblessness among people actively seeking work.

Growth - Increase in the amount of goods and services produced by a nation's resources.

Gross National Product (GNP) - The Value of all goods and services produced by an economic system in one year regardless of where the factors of production are located.

Real Gross National Product - Gross national product adjusted for inflation and changes in the value of a country's currency.

Gross Domestic Product (GDP) - The value of all goods and services produced in a year by a nation's economy through domestic factors of production.

Productivity - Measure of economic growth that compares how much a system with the resources needed to produce it.

Budget deficit - Situation in which a government body spends more money than it takes in.

National debt - Total amount that a nation owes its creditors.

Fiscal policies - Government economic policies that determine how the government collects and spends its revenues.

Monetary policies - Government economic policies that determine the size of a nation's money supply.

TRUE AND FALSE QUESTIONS

1. Disney added a new detention to his theme parks when he discovered that baby boomers had money to spend and the willingness to spend it on themselves.

2. Business is an organization that provides goods or services in order to earn profits.

3. In spite of new technology and international opportunities it is expected that employment will not grow indefinitely.

4. Resources are often called factors of production.

5. Labor includes the physical contributions of people but does not include mental contributions of people as labor.

6. Revenues from the sale of products is an important ongoing source of capital.

7. The most common natural resources are land, water, mineral deposits and trees.

8. A planned economy relies on a centralized government to control all or most factors of production and to make all or most production and allocation decisions.

9. Privatization is the process of converting government enterprises into privately owned companies.

10. The law of demand states that buyers will purchase more of a product as its price drops and less of a product as its price increases.

MULTIPLE CHOICE QUESTIONS

1. Disney created a new demand or the boomer market by:
   a. catering to the trend of shorter vacations
   b. balancing education and entertainment
   c. introducing introductory rates
   d. all of the above

2. Economist say that employment opportunities will grow indefinitely because:
   a. of new forms of technology
   b. growth of service business
   c. growth of international opportunities
   d. all of the above

3. Resources of a country are often called:
   a. factors of production
   b. man's ability to work hard
   c. economic strength
   d. none of the above

4. A country's resources include:
   a. labor
   b. capital
   c. land
   d. all of the above

5. A major source of capital for most smaller businesses is:
   a. the Small Business Administration
   b. personal investments by owner
   c. selling stock in the business
   d. floating bonds in the market

6. In the United States we are a capitalistic country so ownership of businesses are controlled by:
   a. government
   b. stock holders
   c. local communities
   d. nations investors

7. Which country has been known to have a planned economy:
   a. United States
   b. Canada
   c. England
   d. Cuba

8. Market economies that rely on markets not governments to decide what, when and for whom to produce are called:
   a. communistic
   b. capitalistic
   c. socialistic
   d. none of the above

9. Privatization takes place in a country when:
   a. a large corporation takes over a smaller one
   b. stock owners sell their stock to corporations
   c. government sells its enterprises to privately owned companies
   d. none of the above

10. The willingness and ability of buyers to purchase a product, a good or a service is called:
    a. want
    b. need
    c. demand
    d. supply

11. A situation in which the quantity supplied exceeds the quantity demanded is called a:
    a. shortage
    b. surplus
    c. balance economy
    d. none of the above

12. Private enterprise requires the presence of:
    a. private property rights
    b. freedom of choice
    c. profits and competition
    d. all of the above

13. In pure competition:
    a. all firms in a given industry must be small
    b. the number of firms in the industry must be large
    c. no single firm is powerful enough to influence the price of its product.
    d. all of the above

14. An example of an oligopoly is:
    a. American automobile industry
    b. American manufacturing of large commercial aircraft
    c. American oil companies
    d. World production of film

6

15. The biggest threat of stability is:
    a. inflation
    b. prosperity
    c. investments
    d. all of the above

ANSWERS TO TRUE AND FALSE QUESTIONS

1. True   6. True
2. True   7. True
3. False   8. True
4. True   9. True
5. False   10. True

ANSWERS TO MULTIPLE CHOICE QUESTIONS

1 D   6. D   11. B
2. D   7. D   12. D
3. A   8. B   13. D
4. D   9. C   14. B
5. B   10. C   15. A

CHAPTER 2
CONDUCTING BUSINESS IN THE UNITED STATES

CHAPTER OVERVIEW

The English colonist became an integral part of the English trade network, typically selling farm products and raw materials to England and buying manufactured British goods. After the American Revolution, the newly emergent United States began both to expand its own economy and seek new trading partners abroad. With the coming of the Industrial Revolution in the middle of the eighteenth century, a manufacturing revolution was made possible by advances in technology. The U.S. banking system began providing American business with some independence from European capital markets. A great rise in entrepreneur spirit brought the philosophy of laissez-faire. The rise of giant enterprises increased the national standard of living and made U.S. a world power. Scientific management was given impetus with the assembly line concept that increased productivity to near record levels. The production era saw the rise of labor unions and collective bargaining. The marketing era arrives with business determining what customers want before they produce products or services. The global era arrives with products made in the U.S. consumed in world markets and the U.S. importing merchandise from all over the world. Many types of business ownerships sprung up in the U.S. as sole proprietorships, partnerships, cooperatives and corporations were formed. Corporate ownership led to mergers and acquisitions, takeover of competition, corporate alliances and multinational corporations. Government restrictions were soon to follow.

CHAPTER OBJECTIVES

1. Describe the history of business in the United States.

2. Identify the various types of business ownerships.

3. Explain the differences and state the advantages and disadvantages of the sole proprietorship, partnerships and corporations.

4. Describe the differences of a private and a public corporation.

5. Identify three multinational corporations in the U.S.

6. Describe the basic reasons why government made restrictive laws for business.

OPENING VIGNETTE: AVIS TRIES HARDER, SUCCEEDS IN SELLING OUT.

Since Avis, Inc. was founded in 1946 employees found themselves working for eleven different owners. In 1987 the employees became the twelfth owners of Avis through and Employee Stock Ownership Plan (ESOP). Employees owned 71% of the stock and General Motors the remaining 29%. Ownership was originally transferred to employees through a formula that awarded six shares annually for every $1,000 in an individuals salary. Allocations were also based on the percentage of salary diverted to each employee's retirement plan.

Employees were allowed to withdraw some of their shares in cash and those who wanted to retire could also take out cash. This cash drain would have caught ESOP in a cash crunch. In July 1996 HFS offered to buy Avis for $800 million which gave employees three times the per-share value at the end of the year.

Since they were owners, the employees had the knowledge to assess HFS's offer and return to traditional corporate ownership. The decision to sell was based on the financial certainty that would give the ESOP members a financial windfall. One member received over $90,000 on retirement.

This vignette gives another example of the many types of ownership in the U.S. other than sole proprietorships, partnerships and the various types of corporations.

KEY TERMS

Industrial Revolution - Major mid-eighteenth-century change in production characterized by a shift to the factory system, mass production, and the specialization of labor.

Production era - Period during the early twentieth century in which U.S. business focused primarily on improving productivity and manufacturing efficiency.

Marketing concept - Idea that a business must focus on identifying and satisfying consumer wants in order to be profitable.

Sole proprietorship - Business owned and usually operated by one person who is responsible for all of its debts.

Unlimited liability - Legal principle holding owners responsible for paying off all debts of a business.

General partnership - Business with two or more owners who share in both the operation of the firm and in financial responsibility for its debts.

Corporation - Business that is legally considered an entity separate from its owners and is liable for its own debts; owners' liability extends to the limits of their investments.

Public corporation - Corporation whose stock is widely held and available for sale to the general public.

Private corporation - Corporation whose stock is held by a few people and is not available for sale to the general public.

Limited liability - Legal principle holding investors liable for a firm's debts only to the limits of their personal investments in it.

Double taxation - Situation in which taxes may be payable both by a corporation on its profits and by shareholders on dividend incomes.

Corporate governance - Roles of shareholders, directors, and other managers in corporate decision making.

Articles of incorporation - Document detailing the corporate governance of a company, including its name and address, its purpose, and the amount of stock it intends to issue.

Bylaws - Document detailing corporate rules and regulations, including election and responsibilities of directors and procedures for issuing new stock.

Stock - A share of ownership in a corporation.

Stockholder (or **Shareholder**) - An owner of shares of stock in a corporation.

Preferred stock - Stock that guarantees its holders fixed dividends and priority claims over assets but no corporate voting rights.

Common stock - Stock that pays dividends and guarantees corporate voting rights but offers last claims over assets.

Proxy - Authorization granted by a shareholder for someone else to vote his or her shares.

Board of directors - Governing body of a corporation, which reports to its shareholders and delegates power to run its day-to-day operations but remains responsible for sustaining its assets.

Chief Executive Officer (CEO) - Top manager hired by the board of directors to run a corporation.

Merger - The union of two corporations to form a new corporation.

Acquisition - The purchase of one company by another.

Joint venture (or **Strategic alliance**) - Collaboration between two or more organizations on an enterprise.

Employee Stock Ownership Plan (ESOP) - Arrangement in which a corporation holds its own stock in trust for its employees, who gradually receive ownership of the stock and control its voting rights.

Institutional investors - Large investors, such as mutual funds and pension funds, that purchase large blocks of corporate stock.

TRUE AND FALSE QUESTIONS

1. The English Colonist who arrived in North America brought with them the concept of corporation ownership.

2. The industrial revolution replaced hundreds of cottage workers and led them into factories.

3. The rise of giant enterprises increased the poverty of the American worker.

4. The U.S. government has made it a practice not to interfere with American business practices.

5. Henry Ford introduced the moving assembly line and ushered in the production era.

6. Business, government and labor are frequently referred to by economist and politicians as the three "countervailing powers" in society.

7. The marketing concept states "produce what you want and then market aggressively to sell the product".

8. Because of our leadership in technology, American goods can be found all over the world but foreign goods have not as yet made a headway in the U.S.

9. The first form of legal ownership was the partnership.

10. The "hot dog" vendor on the corner of many streets, because of his/ her size cannot become a corporation.

MULTIPLE CHOICE QUESTIONS

1. Two or more owners of a business usually means the business is a:
   a. corporation
   b. sole proprietorship
   c. partnership
   d. cooperative

2. The important benefit of sole proprietorship is:
   a. freedom of running the business
   b. unrestricted assistance from others
   c. large amount of funds available
   d. all of the above

3. One disadvantage of sole proprietorship is:
   a. too much government interference
   b. complicated organizations system needed
   c. legal fees are usually high
   d. none of the above

4. One advantage of sole proprietorship is:
   a. unlimited liability
   b. low start up costs
   c. many owners to help make decisions
   d. taxes are higher

5.   The most common type of partnership is:
        a. general partnership
        b. limited partnership
        c. silent partnership
        d. secret partnership

6.   The striking advantage of general partnerships is:
        a. all partners are liable for each others business debts
        b. their ability to grow with the addition of new money and talent
        c. the fact that they have limited liability
        d. none of the above

7.   A disadvantage of partnership is:
        a. potential lack of continuity
        b. difficulty of transferring ownership
        c. unlimited liability
        d. all of the above

8.   A group of sole proprietorships or partnerships agree to work together for their common benefits is called a:
        a. corporate entity
        b. cooperative
        c. extended ownership
        d. voluntary chain

9.   A corporation may perform the following activity:
        a. sue and be sued
        b. buy, hold land sell property
        c. commit crimes and be punished for them
        d. all of the above

10.   A disadvantage of incorporating is;
        a. difficulty of transferring ownership
        b. unlimited liability
        c. difficulty in raising money
        d. double taxation

11.   The stock that guarantees holders fixed dividends is:
        a. common stock
        b. preferred stock
        c. ancillary stock
        d. all of the above

12. Top managers who have primary responsibility on the corporate board are called :
   a. affiliated directors
   b. outside directors
   c. inside directors
   d. proprietary directors

13. If the A&P Supermarkets and the Red Lion Supermarkets were to merge it would be called a:
   a. vertical merger
   b. horizontal merger
   c. conglomerate merger
   d. none of the above

14. When one firm joins up with another offering the advantage of allowing each firm to remain independent while sharing the risk of a new venture with the other it is called:
   a. corporate alliance
   b. multinational corporation
   c. joint venture
   d. ESOP

ANSWERS TO TRUE AND FALSE QUESTIONS

1. False   6. True
2. True   7. False
3. False   8. False
4. False   9. False
5. True   10. False

ANSWERS TO MULTIPLE CHOICE QUESTIONS

1. C   6. B   11. B
2. A   7. A   12. C
3. D   8. B   13. B
4. B   9. D   14. A
5. A   10. D

CHAPTER 3
UNDERSTANDING THE LEGAL CONTEXT OF BUSINESS

CHAPTER OVERVIEW

Laws are the codified rules of behavior enforced by our society. They fall into three broad categories according to their origins: common, statutory, and regulatory. Laws in the United States originate primarily with English common law. Sources of our law include the Constitution of the U.S. and individual states as well as federal and state statutes. Municipal ordinances, administrative agency rules and regulations, executive orders and court decisions also are sources of our laws. Following precedents lends stability to the law by basing judicial decisions on cases anchored in similar facts. Government agencies and legislation act as a secondary judicial system and determine whether or not regulations have been violated. Agencies have the power to impose penalties. Much of the responsibility for law enforcement falls on the three levels in our court system: federal, state and local. Trial courts are the lowest of the federal court system. Appellate courts hear cases with which the losing party disagrees and the U.S. Supreme Court hears cases appealed from state supreme courts. Business law falls into six basic areas: contract, tort, property, agency, commercial or bankruptcy law. Business law is international and deals with trade agreements, tariffs, patents, copyrights, trademarks and trade secrets.

CHAPTER OBJECTIVES

1. Explain the meaning and basic forms of law.

2. Describe the United States Judicial system.

3. Explain the functions of law.

4. Explain the key legislation that makes up administrative law.

5. Identify and discuss the six major areas of business law.

6. Discuss the international framework of business law.

OPENING VIGNETTE: THE FINE LINE BETWEEN OVERSEEING AND OVERSIGHT

ValuJet Flight 592 crashed into the Florida Everglades on May 11, 1996 killing all 110 people on board. The FAA job is to certify that every U.S. airliner is fit to fly--a mandate that requires rigorous rules and even more rigorous inspection practices. The FAA bowed to the public demand for a hands-off regulatory environment that encourages the growth of low-fare, low-cost start up airlines. A further demand was that safety be a prime factor in inspections.

The FAA followed a policy of "go-easy" for start-up airlines and thus permitted ValuJet to save millions of dollars by farming out its maintenance to foreign countries. Investigations showed that poor communications was evident between the airline and the maintenance company and that improperly sealed oxygen generators set fire to tires stored in the hold. The FAA grounded the airline. ValuJet's rapid growth--including the acquisition of 48 aircraft (eleven different types) in just 31 months and a documented history of safety violations dating back to 1993 was said to be an accident waiting to happen.

The facts uncover a problem of wanting to permit new airlines to get started on a fairly low budget, the requirement of good maintenance (which is costly), and the further requirement that airlines keep to a strict safety standard do not seem to synchronize very well. These are the pressures that the FAA must face. Are accidents the result?

KEY TERMS

Laws - Codified rules of behavior enforced by a society.
Common law - Body of decisions handed down by courts ruling on individual cases.
Statutory law - Law created by constitutions or by federal, state, or local legislative acts.
Regulatory (or Administrative) law - Law made by the authority of administrative agencies.
Deregulation - Elimination of administrative laws and rules that restrict business activity.
Trial court - General court that hears cases not specifically assigned to another court.
Appellate court - Court that reviews case records of trials whose findings have been appealed.
Contract - Any agreement between two or more parties that is enforceable in court.
Capacity - Competence required of individuals entering into a binding contract.
Consideration - Any item of value exchanged between parties to create a valid contract.
Tort - Civil injury to people, property, or reputation for which compensation must be paid.
Intentional tort - Tort resulting from the deliberate actions of a party.
Compensatory damages - Monetary payments intended to redress injury actually suffered because of a tort.
Punitive damages - Fines imposed over and above any actual losses suffered by a plaintiff.
Negligence - Conduct falling below legal standards for protecting others against unreasonable risk.
Product liability tort - Tort in which a company is responsible for injuries caused by its products.

Strict product liability - Principle that liability can result not form a producer's negligence but from a defect in the product itself.

Property - Anything of value to which a person or business has sole right of ownership.

Tangible real property - Land and anything attached to it.

Tangible personal property - Any movable item that can be owned, bought, sold, or, leased.

Intangible personal property - Property that cannot be seen but that exists by virtue of written documentation.

Intellectual property - Property created through a person's creative activities.

Copyright - Exclusive ownership right belonging to the creator of a book, article, design, illustration, photo, film, or musical work.

Trademark - Exclusive legal right to use a brand name or symbol.

Patent - Exclusive legal right to use and license a manufactured item or substance, manufacturing process, or object design.

Eminent domain - Governmental right to claim private land for public use after paying owners fair prices.

Agent - Individual or organization acting for, and in the name of, another party.

Principal - Individual or organization authorizing an agent to act on its behalf.

Express authority - Agent's authority, derived from written agreement, to bind a principal to a certain course of action.

Implied authority - Agent's authority, derived from business custom, to bind a principal To a certain course of action.

Apparent authority - Agent's authority, based on the principal's compliance, to bind a principal to a certain course of action.

Uniform Commercial Code (UCC) - Body of standardized laws governing the rights of buyers and sellers in transactions.

Warranty - Seller's promise to stand by its products or services if a problem occurs after the sale.

Express warranty - Warranty whose terms are specifically stated by the seller.

Implied warranty - Warranty, dictated by law, based on the principle that products should fulfill advertised promises and serve the purposes for which they are manufactured and sold.

Bankruptcy - Permission granted by the courts to individuals and organizations not to pay some or all of their debts.

Involuntary bankruptcy - Bankruptcy proceedings initiated by the creditors of an indebted individual or organization.

Voluntary bankruptcy - Bankruptcy proceedings initiated by an indebted individual or organization.

International law - Set of cooperative agreements and guidelines established by countries to govern actions of individuals, businesses, and nations.

General Agreement on Tariffs and Trade (GATT) - International trade agreement to encourage the multilateral reduction or elimination of trade barriers.

North American Free Trade Agreement (NAFTA) - Agreement to gradually eliminate tariffs and other trade barriers between the United States, Canada, and Mexico.

European Union (EU) - Agreement among major Western European nations to eliminate or make uniform most trade barriers affecting group members.

TRUE AND FALSE QUESTIONS

1. Laws are the codified rule of behavior enforced by a society.

2. There is a three-tier system of courts through which the judicial system administers the law in this country.

3. Common law is not enforceable in American courts.

4. Common law is the basis for all statutory law.

5. Regulatory law is made by the authority of administrative agencies.

6. The Food and Drug Administration is responsible for enduring that food, medicines, and cosmetics are safe and effective.

7. The lowest level of the federal court system is the Appellate courts.

8. You are held liable if you write a proposed contract even if you do not mail or deliver the contract.

9. A person under legal age (usually 18 or 21) cannot enter into a binding contract.

10. If a neighbor offers to paint your house "free of charge" than decides not to do it you can sue him for breach of contract.

MULTIPLE CHOICE QUESTIONS

1. A contract is considered in proper form if it is:
    a. written
    b. oral
    c. implied by conduct
    d. all of the above

2. As the injured party to a breached contract you may take the following action:
    a. cancel the contract and refuse to live up to it
    b. sue for damages
    c. demand specific performance
    d. all of the above

3.   There are___ classification(s) of torts.
        a. 1
        b. 2
        c. 3
        d 4

4.   In the Strict Product Liability law an injured party need show only that:
        a. the product was defective
        b. the products defect was the cause of injury
        c. the defect caused the product to be unreasonably dangerous.
        d. all of the above.

5.   An example of "Real property" is:
        a. a garage
        b. a lawn mower
        c. a car
        d. a TV set

6.   An example of intangible personal property
        a. a built in appliance
        b. an insurance policy
        c. an automobile
        d. a camera

7.   A copyright gives exclusive ownership rights to creators of:
        a. a book
        b. a design
        c. an illustration
        d. all of the above

8.   Trademarks give one exclusive right to use a brand name for:
        a. 10 years
        b. 20 years
        c. 30 years
        d. all of the above

9.   The American Law Institute drew up the Uniform Commercial Code which was accepted by every state except:
        a. New Jersey
        b. Maine
        c. Louisiana
        d. Texas

10. The UCC states that a negotiable instrument must meet certain condition to be legal:
   - a. must be in writing and signed by the issuer
   - b. it must be payable before 60 days
   - c. it must be payable to a specific person only
   - d. it must be notarized by an attorney

11. A business bankruptcy may be resolved by:
   - a. the business ceases to exist
   - b. working out a new payment schedule
   - c. reorganizations with new managers and new strategy
   - d. all of the above

12. A bilateral agreement is one involving:
   - a. only consenting nations
   - b. three or more nations
   - c. two nations
   - d. only nations know to be allies

13. Which of the following determine whether or not regulations have been violated:
   - a. Equal Employment Opportunity Commission
   - b. Food and Drug Administration
   - c. Environmental Protection Agency
   - d. all of the above

14. The appellate Courts consider questions of law, such as possible errors of legal interpretations made by lower courts. Cases are normally heard by:
   - a. a panel of three judges
   - b. a single senior judge
   - c. a panel of two judges
   - d. a panel of four judges

15. A contract made between two or more parties that is enforceable in court need not have:
   - a. agreement of parties
   - b. consent of parties
   - c. capacity of parties
   - d. citizenship of parties

ANSWERS TO TRUE AND FALSE QUESTIONS:

1. True	6. True
2. True	7. False
3. False	8. False
4. False	9. True
5. True	10. False

ANSWERS TO MULTIPLE CHOICE QUESTIONS:

1. D	6. B	11. D
2. D	7. D	12. C
3. C	8. B	13. D
4. D	9. C	14. A
5. A	10. A	15. D

CHAPTER 4
CONDUCTING BUSINESS ETHICALLY AND RESPONSIBLY

CHAPTER OVERVIEW

Ethical behavior affects both internal and external relationships. Business and personal ethics is about what is right and wrong, good or bad. Such behavior conforms to generally accepted social norms concerning beneficial and harmful actions.

Since ethics are based on both social concepts and individual beliefs they vary from person to person as well as from situation to situation. Such behavior is determined partly by the individual and partly by culture. Within a workplace the company itself becomes an additional factor in influencing individual ethical behavior. Many firms establish codes of conduct and develop clear ethical positions on how business should be conducted. Top management must demonstrate support for ethical behavior.

Written codes of behavior and ethics programs have become very important to industry today. Thirty two percent of companies in 1969 had written ethical codes and in 1997 90% of all Fortune 500 firms have such codes.

Most codes are designed to improve standards of both ethical and legal conduct and to aid in self regulation and thus prevent government regulations. They are also designed to increase public confidence in a firm and to show social responsibility. Social responsibility refers to how a business behaves toward other groups and individuals in its social environment: customers, other businesses, employees and investors.

Today's businesses are moving toward enlightened views stressing the need for a greater social role in business. They are aware that unless they correctly handle the environment problems like air, water, and land pollution, recycling and toxic waste disposal, government regulations will get more stringent.

Consumerism is dedicated to protecting the rights of consumers in their dealings with business. Federal and state laws have backed consumer's rights to have a safe product, to be informed of the relevant aspects of the product, have a right to be heard and to choose what they buy.

Unfair pricing, collusion, ethics in advertising and fairness towards employees are all part of the ethics standards. Today we see celebrities who endorse products joining in the fight for ethics in production and have spoken out against unconscionable company activities such as child labor and sweat shop conditions. Improper financial management also plays a big part in the struggle for ethical behavior.

CHAPTER OBJECTIVES

1.   Explain how ethical behavior conforms to generally accepted social norms.

2.   Show how written codes of behavior and ethics programs have become important to industry today.

3.   Explain why most industry codes are designed to improve standards of both ethical and legal conduct.

4.   Explain the forces that help develop individual codes of personal ethics.

5.   Show how consumerism has affected business codes of ethics.

6.   Discuss the importance of ethics in the workplace.

OPENING VIGNETTE: MENDING IMPERFECTIONS IN THE SYSTEM

Three days after a boiler explosion destroyed a privately owned textile company owned by Aaron Feuerstein he announced to the 3,200 employees, that for the next 30 days (or more) they would be paid their full salaries.

Even hardened union members were moved to tears by Feuerstein's social conscience. This came at a very important time when American companies were grappling with the issue of just what companies owe their employees. Feuerstein told his feeling to the Secretary of Labor, and the Senator from Massachusetts during the 1996 State of the Union address. He said that saving the jobs of the hard-working men and women who had contributed so much to his company was the decent and ethical thing to do.

With all the downsizing and layoffs in the nation he hoped this would be the turning of the tide in the treatment of today's workers. Although he was not sure that the insurance would cover the rebuilding of his company he stood fast in his promise to pay the workers.

Mrs. Feuerstein said that her husband's actions were motivated by loyalty and that it never occurred to him not to call back all his workers. He credits his workers with saving the company in the early 1980s, when it was forced into bankruptcy. Rebuilding costs, including the installation of new sophisticated equipment and payments to laid-off workers totaled more than $300 million.

Many workers were back within a week of the fire thanks to the union which agreed to bypass seniority rules and allowed Feuerstein to call workers back according to skills rather than length of service. Less than a month after the fire the mill was producing at 80% of its capacity and within six months all but 500 of the company workers had been recalled.

This vignette shows how a caring company treated its employees both fairly and ethically during a crisis. Ethics in the workplace are becoming increasingly important as we move into an era of intense competition not only for public and consumer support but also for the support of employees and stockholders.

This vignette shows how issues of individual ethics in business and the social responsibility of business affects our economy.

KEY TERMS

Ethics - Beliefs about what is right and wrong or good and bad in actions that affect others.

Ethical behavior - Behavior conforming to generally accepted social norms concerning beneficial and harmful actions.

Social responsibility - The attempt of a business to balance its commitments to groups and individuals in its environment, including customers, other businesses, employees, and investors.

Consumerism - Forms of social activism dedicated to protecting the rights of consumers in their dealing with businesses.

Collusion - Illegal agreement between two or more companies to commit a wrongful act.

Whistleblower - Employee who detects and tries to put an end to a company's unethical, illegal, or socially irresponsible actions by publicizing them.

Check kiting - Illegal practice of writing checks against money that has not yet been credited at the bank on which the checks are drawn.

Social obligation approach - Approach to social responsibility by which a company meets only minimum legal requirements in its commitments to groups and individuals in its social environment.

Social reaction approach - Approach to social responsibility by which a company, if specifically asked to do so, exceeds legal minimums in its commitments to groups and individuals in its social environment.

Social response approach - Approach to social responsibility by which a company actively seeks opportunities to contribute to the well-being of groups and individuals in its social environment.

Social audit - Systematic analysis of a firm's success in using funds earmarked for meeting its social responsibility goals.

TRUE AND FALSE QUESTIONS

1.   Ethics are beliefs about what is right and wrong or good and bad in actions that affects others.

2.   McCall who took over AID in 1993 said that anyone who uses AID in any shape or form or fashion for anything but to help needy nations is wrong

3. What constitutes ethical and unethical behavior is determined mainly by the individual alone.

4. In the workplace companies have little affect in influencing individual ethical behavior.

5. Unfortunately workers determine what is right and wrong and management has little control over these decisions.

6. Today over 90% of all Fortune 500 firms have written ethical codes.

7. Even though business schools must address the issue of ethics in the workplace, companies must take the chief responsibility for educating employees.

8. Social responsibility does not refer to the way in which a business behaves toward other groups or individuals, social responsibility deals with individuals only.

9. Demands of investors and competition does not play a part in shaping a company's ethics.

10. No toy company would ever think of refusing to sell toy guns because they look too realistic.

MULTIPLE CHOICE QUESTIONS

1. Aaron Feuerstein guaranteed the workers salaries even though the factory was destroyed because:
    a. he was concerned about violence if he did not
    b. he felt it was the right thing to do
    c. the union demanded it
    d. all of the above

2. Erly was unethical in his relationship with AID because:
    a. he reinvested proceeds from its low-cost government loan back in the U.S. at higher rates.
    b. he exploited political connections
    c. he loosely managed government programs
    d. all of the above

3. We learn our ethics from:
    a. parent
    b. school
    c. friends
    d. all of the above

4. Written codes are not designed to perform one function:
    a. increase public confidence in the firm
    b. to be eligible for governmental "Behavioral Tax Reduction"
    c. to stem the tide of government regulations
    d. to respond to problems that arise as a result of unethical or illegal behavior

5. Levi Strauss & Co. addresses a number of issues in its "Aspiration Statement" but not:
    a. work-force diversity
    b. employee empowerment and recognition
    c. pay for the work force
    d. honest communications

6. Social responsibility refers to the way in which a business behaves toward:
    a. other groups in a social environment
    b. investors
    c. customers
    d. all of the above

7. Four areas of concern: responsibilities toward the environment, its customers, its employees, and its investors is called a company's:
    a. area of social responsibility
    b. sales promotion idea
    c. lack of concern for investors profits
    d. hidden agenda

8. American industry must be concerned with pollution especially pollution of:
    a. air
    b. water
    c. land
    d. all of above

9. U.S. manufacturers produce___million tons of toxic waste each year.
    a. 2 to 10
    b. 20 to 30
    c. 40 to 60
    d. none of the above

10. The Environmental Protection Agency (EPA), an independent federal agency charged with protecting resources and encouraging conservation, administers the program under which the following pay a special tax that goes to restoring polluted land to its natural state:
    a. retail and wholesale food distributors
    b. chemical and oil companies
    c. all manufacturers
    d. all handlers of liquid materials

11. The Federal Trade Commission regulates:
   a. uniformity of product quality
   b. guidelines for pharmaceutical
   c. labeling of food products
   d. advertising and pricing policies

12. What influenced most the rapid decision of American firms to pull British beef off their shelves because of "Mad Cow Disease" was it:
   a. America anxiety about litigation
   b. value of maintaining consumer confidence
   c. American emphasis on health concerns
   d. beef can be gotten cheaper in the U.S. anyway

13. Recently a law was passed that made it mandatory that the slats spaces in baby cribs be closer together to prevent baby strangulation. Which of the following had to do with the law:
   a. consumers right to a safe product
   b. consumers right to be informed about all relevant
      aspects of a product
   c. consumers right to be heard
   d. consumers right to choose what they buy

14. An example of collusion is when:
   a. hospitals and local physicians agree on what prices various hospital services
      would cost
   b. neighboring universities agree on tuition rates between themselves
   c. three supermarkets join together to become one
      new company
   d. a and b only

15. Whistle-blowers are those employees
   a. responsible to sound the horn that work should begin
   b. government agencies hire to uncover illegal act of any company
   c. an employee who informs the authorities of illegal acts of his company
   d. an employee who is hired by the company to uncover illegal acts of the
      company

ANSWERS TO TRUE AND FALSE QUESTIONS

1. True   6. True
2. True   7. True
3. False   8. False
4. False   9. False
5. False   10. False

26

ANSWERS TO MULTIPLE CHOICE QUESTIONS

1. B	6. D	11. D
2. D	7. A	12. B
3. D	8. D	13. A
4. B	9. C	14. D
5. C	10. B	15. C

CHAPTER 5
UNDERSTANDING THE GLOBAL CONTEXT OF BUSINESS

CHAPTER OVERVIEW

The total volume of world trade today is immense--around $7 trillion each year. Foreign investment in the United States alone is approaching $1 trillion, while direct investment abroad by U.S. firms has already passed the $1 trillion mark. The world is fast becoming a single independent system called globalization.

To be considered a truly global economy basic facts must be present: an international trade in goods and services, movement of labor, the flow of money moved internationally and the international flow of information.

Information technology will be the centerpiece of the new global economy, and the growth in the service sector will help to fuel its development. The world marketplace today revolves around three major marketplaces: North America, Western Europe, and the Pacific Rim. The United States dominates the North American business region. Europe is often divided into two regions, Western Europe dominated by Germany, the United Kingdom, France and Italy. Eastern Europe which was until recently primarily communistic has gained in importance. This includes Russia, Poland and neighboring countries.

The Pacific rim is an important force in the world economy and a major source of competition for North America. Japan, South Korea, Taiwan and Hong Kong produce a great supply of merchandise for the United States. China the most densely populated country in the world, continues to emerge as an important market in its own right.

A nation's balance of trade is the total economic value of all products that it imports minus the total economic value of all products that it exports. When a country's imports exceed its exports--it has a negative balance of trade and suffers a trade deficit. Balance of payments refers to the flow of money into or out of a country.

The balance of imports and exports between two countries is affected by the exchange rate differences in their currencies. An exchange rate is the rate at which the currency of one nation can be exchanged for that of another. Floating exchange rates are the norm when the value of one country's currency relative to that of another varies with market conditions. When a dollar is stronger in relation to another country's currency the price of goods falls in the U.S. and rises in the other country.

If there is international demand for its product, a firm must consider whether and how to adapt that product to meet the special demands of foreign customers. After a firm decides to go international it must decide on the level of its international involvement. An exporter is a firm that makes products in one country and then distributes them in others, while an importer buys products in foreign countries and resells them in his home country.

An international firm conducts a significant portion of its business in foreign countries. Multinational firms do their planning and decision making geared to international markets. An independent agent is a foreign individual or organization who agrees to represent an exporter's interest in foreign markets. Some companies sign licensing arrangements which gives them exclusive rights to manufacture or market their products in that market and they pay royalties for the license.

One must deal with economic difference, legal and political difference, quotas, tariffs and subsidies in international trade. Some countries participate in dumping, that is selling a product abroad for less than the comparable price charged at home. Many countries make this process illegal because it gives the exporter a great advantage on the host country.

CHAPTER OBJECTIVES

1. Explain international business and identify the major world marketplaces.

2. Describe how economic, legal, social, cultural and political differences among nations affect international business.

3. Explain the differences between absolute advantage and comparative advantage.

4. Describe how a tariff differs from an embargo.

5. Explain how the exchange rate of a country can affect the balance of trade.

OPENING VIGNETTE: FOR A FEW DOLLARS MORE

Selling software to Chinese consumers is not quite as natural to Bill Gates as selling here in the U.S. but it is becoming an increasingly important facet of Microsoft's business strategy. Every year, illegal factories in the People's Republic manufacture 54 million bogus software packages robbing Microsoft and other firms of revenue rightfully theirs. These sales are called pirating.

The pirating of merchandise has actually helped Microsoft in a way because more Chinese use the pirated computers and more are getting to understand the need for computers. Therefore, Microsoft is selling more software to the new purchasers. It is expected that more than 5 million computers will be sold in China by the year 2000.

The Chinese government itself is buying more and more computers to monitor the collection of new taxes planned on the computer owners. Microsoft has developed a Chinese-language Windows operating system and is collaborating with Chinese researchers to develop speech recognition and handwriting analysis software so that they can utilize the difficult Chinese characters on a keyboard.

In order to do business in foreign countries a company has to be able to adjust its manufacturing to that country's needs and may actually set up manufacturing plants in those foreign countries. This vignette shows how far a company will go in order to open up the doors of trade with a country offering a promising future.

KEY TERMS

Globalization - Process by which the world economy is becoming a single interdependent economic system.

Import - Product made or grown abroad but sold domestically.

Export - Product made or grown domestically but shipped and sold abroad.

Absolute advantage - The ability to produce something more efficiently than any other country can.

Comparative advantage - The ability to produce some products more efficiently than others.

Balance of trade - Economic value of all products a country imports minus the economic value of all the products it imports.

Trade deficit - Situation in which a country's imports exceed its exports, creating a negative balance of trade.

Trade surplus - Situation in which a country's exports exceed its imports, creating a positive balance of trade.

Balance of payments - Flow of all money into or out of a country.

Exchange rate - Rate at which the currency of one nation can be exchanged for the currency of another country.

International firm - Firm that conducts a significant portion of its business in foreign countries.

Multinational firm - Firm that designs, produces, and markets products in many nations.

Independent agent - Foreign individual or organization that agrees to represent an exporter's interests.

Licensing arrangement - Arrangement in which firms choose foreign individuals or organizations to manufacture or market their products in another country.

Royalty - Payment made to a license holder in return for the right to market the licenser's product.

Branch office - Foreign office set up by an international or multinational firm.

Strategic alliance (or **Joint venture**) - Arrangement in which a company finds a foreign partner to contribute approximately half of the resources needed to establish and operate a new business in the partner's country.

Direct investment - Arrangement in which a firm buys or establishes tangible assets in another country.

Quota - Restriction on the number of products of a certain type that can be imported into a country.

Embargo - Government order banning exportation and/or importation of a particular product of all products from a particular country.

Tariff - Tax levied on imported products.

Subsidy - Government payment to help a domestic business compete with foreign firms.

Protectionism - Practice of protecting domestic business against foreign competition.

Local content law - Law requiring that products sold in a particular country be at least partly made there.

Business practice laws - Laws or regulations governing business practices in given countries.

Cartel - Association of producers whose purpose is to control supply and prices.

Dumping - Practice of selling a product for less than the cost of production.

TRUE AND FALSE QUESTIONS

1. The total of world trade today is around $2 billion.

2. Globalization takes place when the world economy becomes a single interdependent system.

3. The contemporary world economy revolves around three major marketplaces.

4. Eastern Europe which until recently was part of the communist world, has still not gained a place in that areas marketplace.

5. Balance of payments refers to the flow of money into or out of a country.

6. If the dollar were stronger in relation to the franc, the prices of all American-made products would rise in France.

7. A exporter is a firm that makes products in one country and then distributes and sells them in others.

8. An international firm in America may not conduct a significant portion of its business in foreign countries.

9. It is relatively difficult for American companies starting international operations to locate agents, develop sales agreements and begin exporting.

10. Anyone American planning to conduct business in another country usually understands business is business and the host's society and culture usually are the same as ours.

MULTIPLE CHOICE QUESTIONS

1. A well-known Japanese strategy for keeping foreign goods out of the home market is by:
    a. overproducing the same item in Japan
    b. finding excessive fault with them
    c. forcing the foreign country to "dump" goods in Japan
    d. none of the above

2. A quota on goods of a foreign country:
    a. restricts the total number of products of a certain type
    b. adds a tax on all items imported
    c. forbids any goods to be imported
    d. raises the price of the imported goods

3. A tariff on goods of a foreign country:
    a. restricts the total number of products of a certain type
    b. adds a tax on all items imported
    c. forbids any goods to be imported
    d. raises the price of the imported goods

4. A subsidy is something a government does to:
    a. restrict domestic business
    b. tax foreign imports
    c. help a domestic business compete
    d. none of the above

5 Dumping is:
    a. selling the product abroad at a much higher price than at the home country
    b. getting rid of the merchandise that is inferior or damaged
    c. selling a product abroad for less than at home
    d. profitable for the importing country

6. MIT professor Krugman has identified some basic facets of a truly global economy they are:
    a. an international trade of goods
    b. a lesser international trade in services
    c. an international movement of labor
    d. all of the above

7. The value of all goods and services produced domestically by a nation each year is called:
    a. gross national profit
    b. gross domestic product
    c. gross national product
    d. gross national income

8. The Pacific Rim consists of these three and more:
    a. Japan, China and Korea
    b. Japan, Germany and China
    c. Russia, Japan and Taiwan
    d. Indonesia, India and Hong Kong

9. The major financial center in the Pacific Rim is:
    a. North Korea
    b. Taiwan
    c. Hong Kong
    d. South Korea

10. When a country can produce something more cheaply than any other country it is said to have:
    a. absolute advantage
    b. a comparative advantage
    c. advantage of child labor and low wages
    d. lower taxes

11 The total economic value of all products that it imports minus the total economic value of all products that it exports is called the:
    a. profit ratio
    b. balance of trade
    c. balance of payments
    d. country's deficit

12 The U.S. dollar grew in strength in the foreign market because U.S. businesses succeeded in reducing:
    a. unemployment
    b. inflation
    c. the budget deficit
    d. all the above

13. Multinational firm headquarters location are usually:
    a. in America
    b. in United Nations building
    c. where most sales originate
    d. irrelevant

14. Independent agents are foreign individuals who:
    a. agree to represent an exporter
    b. sells the exporter's products
    c. collects payment for exporter
    d. all of above

15. Firms that give individuals or companies in a foreign country exclusive rights to manufacture or market their products in that market are called:
        a. vendors
        b. wholesalers
        c. licensees
        d. middle-men

ANSWERS TO TRUE AND FALSE QUESTIONS

1. False	6. True
2. True	7. True
3. True	8. False
4. False	9. False
5. True	10. False

ANSWERS TO MULTIPLE CHOICE QUESTIONS

1. B	6. D	11. B
2. A	7. B	12. D
3. B	8. A	13. D
4. C	9. C	14. D
5. C	10. A	15. C

CHAPTER 6
MANAGING THE BUSINESS ENTERPRISE

CHAPTER OVERVIEW

The starting point in effective management is setting goals-objectives that a business hopes to achieve. Managers make decisions about actions that will and will not achieve company goals. A broad program underlies these decisions. That program is called strategy.

Strategy formulation begins with setting goals for an organization. Goal setting provides direction and guidance for managers at all levels. Goal setting helps firms allocate resources and helps to define corporate culture. Goal setting also helps managers assess performance of units under the managers control.

Goals differ according to a firms purpose. The mission statement states how it will achieve its purpose. Regardless of the company's purpose and mission every firm needs long term, intermediate and short time goals. Long term goals relate to extended periods of time, five years or more. Intermediate goals are set for a period of one to five years and short term goals are set for one year.

The board of directors of a firm usually set the goals and its mission. Top managers usually set long term goals and middle managers act to set short term goals.

Strategy formulation involves three basic steps, setting strategic goals, analyzing the organization and environment and matching the organization and its environment. Strategic goals are long term goals and are derived from the firms mission statement.

The heart of strategy formulation is the matching of environmental threats and opportunities against corporate strengths and weaknesses.

Plans are viewed on three levels: strategic, tactical and operational. Strategic plans reflect decisions about resource allocations, company priorities and steps needed to meet strategic goals. Tactical plans are shorter-range plans for implementing specific aspects of the company's strategic plans. Operational plans set short term targets for daily, weekly, or monthly performance

Contingency planning is planning for change while crisis management involves an organization's methods of dealing with emergencies. The management process deals with planning, organizing, directing, and controlling an organization's financial, physical, human and information resources to achieve its goals. The three basic levels of management are top, middle, and first-line. Top managers set general policies, middle management is responsible to implement the strategies and first line managers work directly with the production force.

Human resource managers hire, train, evaluate employee performance and determine compensation. Operational managers are responsible for production, inventory and quality control. Marketing managers are responsible for getting products from producers to consumers and information managers design and implement systems to gather, organize and distribute information.

Financial managers plan and oversee accounting functions and financial resources of a company. All managers must have managerial skills. The skills needed to perform specialized tasks are called technical skills. Those needed to understand others and motivate workers are called human relation skills.

Conceptual skills refer to a person's ability to think in the abstract, to diagnose and analyze different situations and see beyond the present situation. Decision making skills include the ability to define the problems and select the best course of action.

Tomorrow's managers must equip themselves with the special tools, techniques and skills necessary to compete in a global environment. Corporate culture is shaped by values of top management, a firms history, and its shared experiences.

CHAPTER OBJECTIVES

1. Explain the importance of setting goals and formulating strategies.

2. Explain long term, intermediate and short term goals.

3. Describe the three basic steps of strategy formulation.

4. Explain the level and area of different types of managers.

5. Describe the various formulating aspects of corporate culture.

6. Identify and explain the three levels of the hierarchy of plans.

OPENING VIGNETTE: IF THE SHOE VIRTUALLY FITS

Jeffrey Silverman worked selling shoes since he was sixteen years old and came to the conclusion that shoe stores sold customers what they carried in inventory rather than what customers wanted. Since inventory carries a heavy investment, some stores do not want to carry the inventory needed to keep customers happy.

He set up a store (Custom Foot) with only 150 samples on display to show customers how shoes look but not how they feel on their feet. Customers have their feet measured by an electronic scanner which measures the foot in 14 different ways. A salesperson helps the customer choose the specific style, color, grade of leather, lining and so on from the store's "virtual inventory". Specially designed software translates the customers choices into an order, which is faxed to Italy and the shoe is made. So many customers are willing to wait a short period of time to get exacting fit that his store in Westport, Connecticut took in $4 million to $7 million in its first year. By the end of 1997 he is expected to have opened 100 stores nationwide. His next move is to open stores in podiatrist offices.

This case illustrates how an entrepreneur who recognized a need, a challenge and an opportunity, utilized good business skills to run a business. This vignette also illustrates how setting goals, and formulating strategies can lead to a successful business and how a small business depends on effective management.

KEY TERMS

Goal - Objective that a business hopes and plans to achieve.

Mission statement - Organization's statement of how it will achieve its purpose in the environment in which it conducts its business.

Long-term goals - Goals set for extended periods of time, typically five years or more into the future.

Intermediate goals - Goals set for a period of one to five years into the future.

Short-term goals - Goals set for the very near future, typically less that one year.

Strategy formulation - Creation of a broad program for defining and meeting an organization's goals.

Strategic goals - Long-term goals derived directly from a firm's mission statement.

Environmental analysis - Process of scanning the business environment for threats and opportunities.

Organizational analysis - Process of analyzing a firm's strengths and weaknesses.

Strategic plans - Plans reflecting decisions about resource allocations, company priorities, and steps needed to meet strategic goals.

Tactical plans - Generally short-range plans concerned with implementing specific aspects of a company's strategic plans.

Operational plans - Plans setting short-term targets for daily, weekly, or monthly performances.

Management - Process of planning, organizing, directing, and controlling an organization's resources in order to achieve its goals.

Planning - Management process of determining what an organization needs to do and how best to get it done.

Organizing - Management process of determining how best to arrange an organization's resources and activities into a coherent structure.

Directing - Management process of guiding and motivating employees to meet an organization's objectives.

Controlling - Management process of monitoring an organization's performance to ensure that it is meeting its goals.

Top managers - Managers responsible to the board of directors and stockholders for a firm's overall performance and effectiveness.

Middle managers - Managers responsible for implementing the strategies, policies, and decisions made by top managers.

First-line managers - Managers responsible for supervising the work of employees.

Technical skills - Skills needed to perform specialized tasks.

Human relations skills - Skills in understanding and getting along with people.

Conceptual skills - Abilities to think in the abstract, diagnose and analyze different situations, and see beyond the present situation.

Decision-making skills - Skills in defining problems and selecting the best courses of action.

Time management skills - Skills associated with the productive use of time.

Corporate culture - The shared experiences, stories, beliefs, and norms that characterize an organization.

TRUE AND FALSE QUESTIONS

1. Principles of management apply to businesses but do not relate to managers in other institutions like charities, educational institutions and government.

2. The starting point in effective management is setting goals.

3. A mission statement tells how it will achieve its purpose in the environment in which it conducts its business.

4. The board of directors of a firm generally sets long and short term goals.

5. Environmental analysis in management involves the examination for toxic wastes and air pollution in a company.

6. Management is the process of planning, organizing, directing and controlling an organization.

7. Directing is the process of monitoring a firm's performance to make sure that it is meeting its goals.

8. Operational managers are responsible for production, inventory and quality control.

9. Skill needed to perform specialize tasks are called conceptual skills.

10. The values of top management usually set the tone for an organization.

MULTIPLE CHOICE QUESTIONS

1. The starting point in effective management is:
   a. setting goals
   b. setting strategy
   c. selling stocks for finances
   d. hiring human relation experts

2. Long term goals are set for:
   a. one year
   b. two to three years
   c. five years or more
   d. undetermined amount of years

3. Strategy formulation involves :
   a. setting strategic goals
   b. analyzing the organization and its environment
   c. Matching the organization and its environment
   d. all of the above

4. Environmental analysis involves scanning the environment for threats and opportunities. Threats to be considered are:
   a. changing consumer tastes
   b. hostile takeover offers
   c. new government regulations
   d. all of the above

5. Organizational analysis is made to better understand a company's strengths and weaknesses. Strengths to be considered are:
   a. surplus cash
   b. dedicated work force
   c. little competition
   d. all of the above

6. Decisions about resource allocation, company priorities and steps need to meet strategic goals are important in:
   a. tactical planning
   b. strategic planning
   c. contingency planning
   d. all of the above

7.	In the hierarchy of plans, plans can be viewed on three levels that logically flow from one level to the next. The first level is:
	a. strategic
	b. tactical
	c. operational
	d. functional

8.	The plan that sets short-term targets for daily, weekly, or monthly performance is:
	a. strategic plans
	b. tactical plans
	c. operational plans
	d. functional plans

9.	The planning that is a hedge against changes that might occur and thus is planning for a change is called:
	a. strategic plans
	b. contingency plans
	c. executive plans
	d. none of the above

10.	The managing process includes:
	a. planning
	b. organizing
	c. directing
	d. all of the above

11.	The manager responsible for implementing the strategies, policies, and decisions made by top managers is the:
	a. middle manager
	b. first-line manager
	c. operations manager
	d. none of the above

12.	The manager responsible to hire and train employees, to evaluate performance and to determine compensation is the:
	a. operations manager
	b. human resource manager
	c. marketing manager
	d. financial manager

13. The skill that refer to a person's ability to think in the abstract, to diagnose analyze different situations, and to see beyond the present situation is categorized as one with:
    a. human relation skills
    b. conceptual skills
    c. decision making skills
    d. time-management skills

14. A strong corporate culture serves a purpose:
    a. it directs employees' efforts and helps everyone work toward the same goals.
    b. it helps newcomers learn accepted behaviors
    c. it gives each organization its own identity, much as personality gives identity to people
    d. all of the above

15. Financial managers are involved in the firms:
    a. borrowing of monies
    b. checking credit of customers
    c. financial resources
    d. all of the above

ANSWERS TO TRUE AND FALSE QUESTIONS

1. False   6. True
2. True   7. False
3. True   8. True
4. False   9. False
5. False   10. True

ANSWERS TO THE MULTIPLE CHOICE QUESTIONS

1. A   6. B   11. A
2. C   7. A   12. B
3. D   8. C   13. D
4. D   9. B   14. D
5. D   10. D   15. D

CHAPTER 7
ORGANIZING THE BUSINESS ENTERPRISE

CHAPTER OVERVIEW

Each organization has the same fundamental purpose to succeed and earn a profit. Each must develop its own appropriate organization structure. A variety of important factors come into play when determining this structure. A dynamic and rapidly growing enterprise needs an organization with flexibility and growth possibilities. A stable organization with only modest growth will naturally function best with a different structure.

Size, technology, and changes in environmental circumstances affect structure. Most organizations change their structure on an almost continuing basis. Most businesses prepare organization charts to clarify structure and to show employees where they fit into a firms operation. The first step in developing the structure of any business is to determine who will do what (specialization). The second is (departmentalizing) concerned with how people performing certain tasks can best be grouped together.

Job specialization identifies the specific jobs that need to be done. After jobs have been specialized they are grouped into logical unit called departmentalization. Departmentalization may occur along customer, product, process, geographic or functional lines.

The making of decision hierarchy results from a three step process: assigning tasks, performing tasks and distributing authority. Responsibility is the duty to perform an assigned task and authority is the power to make the decisions necessary to complete the task. Delegation begins when a manager assigns a task to a subordinate and accountability falls to the subordinate who must then complete the task.

In a centralized organization most decision-making authority is held by upper level managers. Most lower-level decisions must be approved by upper management. As a company gets larger it has a tendency to adopt a decentralized organization. Authority is delegated to levels of management at various points below the top.

The number of people managed by one supervisor is called the manager's span of control. A wide span of control is given for simple tasks under one supervisor. When jobs are more diversified or prone to change, a narrow span of control is preferable.

In the three forms of authority, line authority is usually linked to the production and sales of specific products. Staff authority is based on special expertise and usually involves counseling and advising line managers. Committee and team authority has committees and teams play an important role in daily operations.

Functional organization is structured around basic business functions-marketing, operations, finance and so forth, each with its own department. Divisional organization relies on product departmentalization which operates as a relatively autonomous business under the larger corporate umbrella. In a matrix structure, teams are formed in which individuals report to two or more managers. Many times this arrangement is temporary and installed to complete a specific project, then disbanded.

All the above areas are involved in formal structure but firms also utilize informal structure. The informal organization takes place during everyday social interactions among employees. This transcends formal jobs and job interrelationships and effectively alters a company's formal structure. Informal structure may reinforce office politics that puts interests of individuals ahead of that of the firm.

CHAPTER OBJECTIVES

1.   Explain the elements that influences a firm's organizational structure.

2.   Differentiate between specialization and departmentalization.

3.   Show how responsibility and authority differ.

4.   Discuss the differences between delegation and authority.

5.   Identify the differences between formal and informal organization.

OPENING VIGNETTE:
UNITED AIRLINES GIVES MANAGERS THE POWER TO MANAGE

A team made up of pilots, ramp workers, and managers sat down together for the first time to figure out how to power planes idling at the gate, with electricity, instead of jet fuel. Electricity would save money, but because their short working ladders prevented ramp workers from plugging electric cables into the aircraft, it was literally out of reach. The solution was to get longer ladders, and some of them actually knew the solution but each was in his own specialty location and never communicated to the other.

Pilots were only concerned with the piloting of the airplane. The ramp worker with his problem, etc. Authority was so decentralized that each knew what was going on in their own specialty only. When the group got together to discuss the problem, they shared their knowledge with each other and came up with a very easy solution. They recommended the company buy bigger ladders so as to be able to connect the electrical wires into the electricity and power the motors with electricity.

The group, meeting together, were able to see how their problems related to other departmental problems and for the first time were able to come up with a solution to satisfy everyone. This vignette shows the importance of flexibility in management and how the group working together as a team can solve what seemed to be an insurmountable problem.

KEY TERMS

Organizational structure - Specification of the jobs to be done within an organization and the ways in which they relate to one another.

Organizational chart - Diagram depicting a company's structure and showing employees where they fit into its operations

Chain of command - Reporting relationships within a company.

Job specialization - The process of identifying the specific jobs that need to be done and designating the people who will perform them.

Departmentalization - Process of grouping jobs into logical units.

Profit center - Separate company unit responsible for its own costs and profits.

Customer departmentalization - Departmentalization according to types of customers likely to buy a given product.

Product departmentalization - Departmentalization according to products being created.

Process departmentalization - Departmentalization according to production process used to create a good or services.

Geographic departmentalization - Departmentalization according to areas served by a business.

Functional departmentalization - Departmentalization according to functions or activities.

Responsibility - Duty to perform an assigned task.

Authority - Power to make the decisions necessary to complete a task.

Delegation - Assignment of a task, a responsibility or authority by a manager to a subordinate.

Accountability - Liability of subordinates for accomplishing tasks assigned by managers.

Centralized organizations - Organization in which most decision-making authority is held by upper-level management.

Decentralized organizations - Organization in which a great deal of decision-making authority is delegated to levels of management at points below the top.

Span of control - Number of people supervised by one manager.

Line authority - Organizational structure in which authority flows in a direct chain of command from the top of the company to the bottom.

Line department - Department directly linked to the production and sales of a specific product.

Staff authority - Authority that is based on expertise and that usually involves advising line managers.

Staff members - Advisers and counselors who aid line departments in making decisions but do not have the authority to make final decisions.

Committee and team authority - Authority granted to committees or work teams involved in a firm's daily operations.

✓Functional organization - Form of business organization in which authority is determined by the relationships between group functions and activities.

✓Divisional organization - organizational structure in which corporate divisions operate as relatively autonomous businesses under the large corporate umbrella.

Division - Department that resembles a separate business in producing and marketing its own products.

✓Matrix structure - Organizational structure in which teams are formed and team members report to two or more managers.

International organizational structures - Approaches to organizational structure developed in response to the need to manufacture, purchase, and sell in global markets.

Informal organization - Network, unrelated to the firm's formal authority structure, of everyday social interactions among company employees.

Intrapreneuring - Process of creating and maintaining the innovation and flexibility of a small business environment within the confines of a large organization.

TRUE AND FALSE QUESTIONS

1. The United States has been transformed from a top-driven hierarchical organization into one that values teamwork, initiative, and creativity. *True*

2. We define organizational structure as the specifications of the jobs to be done within an organization and the ways in which those jobs relate to one another. *True*

3. Once organizational structure is in place a well run company will resist changing its structure. *False*

4. Job specialization has to do with preparing the majority of the workers to be familiar with all jobs to be done in a plant. *False*

5. Departmentalization allows the firm to treat a department as a profit center responsible for its own costs and profits. *True*

6. In a matrix structure teams are formed permanently to do continuous work together. *False*

7. Informal organization can reinforces office politics that put the interest of individuals ahead of those of the firm. *True*

8. Intrapreneuring creates and maintains the innovation and flexibility of a small business environment within the confines of a large, bureaucratic structure. *True*

9. Span of control refers to the number of people who work for any individual manager. *True*

10. In areas where both line and line and staff systems are involved, the line departments generally have authority to give advise only. *False*

MULTIPLE CHOICE QUESTIONS

1. Organization structure is often affected by:
   - a. size
   - b. technology
   - c. changes in environmental circumstances
   - **d. all of the above**

2. Most companies prepare organization charts to:
   - a. clarify structure
   - b. show employees where they fit in
   - c. better organize management
   - **d. all of the above**

3. The first step in developing the structure of any business is to:
   - **a. determine who will do what**
   - b. determine where the priority jobs are located
   - c. make a competitive comparison in the market place'
   - d. none of the above

4. The process of identifying the specific jobs that need to be done and designating the people who will perform them leads to:
   - a. job specification
   - **b. job specialization**
   - c. job description
   - d. none of the above

5. A profit center is:
   - a. a unit that makes a profit
   - **b. a unit responsible for its own cost and profit**
   - c. a new unit carrying high mark-up merchandise
   - d. a department where profits are hoped for

6. Customer departmentalization makes shopping easier because:
   - a. it provides identifiable store segments
   - b. sales people know more about the merchandise
   - c. departments can be placed near related merchandise
   - **d. all of the above**

7. Functional departmentalization usually takes place on which level:
   - **a. top level**
   - b. middle level
   - c. production level
   - d. is never located at any level

8. When a president delegates a task to a top manager, who then delegates it to his on-line manger, who delegates it to a worker on the line and the task is never completed who must answer to the president:
    a. the worker on the line
    b. the line manger
    c. the top manager
    d. all of them

9. In a centralized organization, most decision-making is held by:
    a. upper-level managers
    b. lower-level managers
    c. on-line workers
    d. all of the above

10. The manager's span of control depends on:
    a. employee abilities
    b. payroll considerations
    c. item being manufactured
    d. number of people working in the plant

11. An example of a worker considered a staff authority would be:
    a. a on-line computer worker
    b. a firms lawyer
    c. a on-line production worker
    d. none of the above

12. The atomic manager model described in the text requires managers who are:
    a. the kind to upset and right the apple cart
    b. democratic managers
    c. lais-sez faire manger
    d. dictatorial managers

13. Companies free to buy, sell, create, and disband divisions without disrupting the rest of their operations are made up of which kind of organization
    a. functional organization
    b. divisional organization
    c. centralized organization
    d. decentralized organization

14. A temporary measure, installed to complete a specific project and affecting only one part of the firm is an example of:
    a. functional organization
    b. divisional organization
    c. matrix organization
    d. international organization

15. When the workers of the company join in to buy majority control of the company it is called:
    - (a) employee stock-ownership
    - b. mutual stock ownership
    - c. unionized ownership
    - d. none of the above

ANSWERS TO TRUE AND FALSE QUESTIONS

1. True	6. False
2. True	7. True
3. False	8. True
4. False	9. True
5. True	10. False

ANSWERS TO MULTIPLE CHOICE QUESTIONS

1. D	6. D	11. B
2. D	7. A	12. A
3. A	8. A	13. B
4. B	9. A	14. C
5. B	10. A	15. A

CHAPTER 8
UNDERSTANDING ENTREPRENEURSHIP AND THE SMALL BUSINESS

CHAPTER OVERVIEW

There are many definitions of small business but the one most people accept is: an independently owned and managed business that does not dominate its market. Most U.S. workers are employed by small business and most U.S. businesses employ less than 1,000 employees.

In the 1980's small business created eight out of every ten new jobs in the U.S. Today the 80% has dropped somewhat but continues to be a major factor in employment. Business success, more than business size accounts for most new-job creation. Small businesses hire at twice the rate as large ones, but they also eliminate jobs at a much higher rate.

Most of the products of big manufacturers are sold to consumers by small businesses. The five major small businesses are services, retailing, wholesaling, manufacturing and agriculture. Manufacturing is the most difficult business to start and services the easiest.

Entrepreneurs make up the bulk of small business. Most successful entrepreneurs have a strong desire to be their own boss, are not afraid of hard work, and enjoy taking a risk. The so called Generation X, those people between 25 and 34 years of age start their own businesses at a rate three times higher than any other age group.

Failures in new enterprises are declining and now 77% of new start-ups remain in operation for at least three years, but 60% will not celebrate a sixth anniversary. Opportunities for minorities and women and new opportunities in global enterprises has improved the rate of survival among small business. On-line commerce gives small business nearly the same ability as large corporations to reach a global market.

Four general factors contribute to small business failure: managerial incompetence or inexperience, neglect, weak control systems and insufficient funds. Factors that contribute to success in small business: hard work, drive and dedication, market demand for the product, managerial competence and luck.

An entrepreneur must decide whether he/she wants to buy an existing business or build from the ground up. The latter form is more risky since there is no customer base in which to start. The best way to gain knowledge about a business is to work in it

before deciding to open your own business. Obtaining finances can be a problem but a wide variety of monetary resources are available from private to governmental agencies. Venture capital firms and small business investment companies are other sources of investment. The Small Business Administration (SBA) has a number of plans to help the small business person. Advisory boards and management consultants can be "advice" givers and the SBA has a number of free services for the small business person.

Franchising can also be a good way to start ones business. The franchiser may train the franchisee, pick the location, negotiate the lease, design the store and purchase necessary equipment but becomes a "partner" for the life of the agreement. Franchising has grown in all fields from fast food, the automobile rentals to pharmacies and motels. While they do minimize risk they do not guarantee success.

CHAPTER OBJECTIVES

1. Explain the importance of small business in the U.S.

2. Define small business using the SBA definition.

3. Differentiate between franchiser and franchisee

4. Explain what types of small business are most successful

5. Define entrepreneurship and the characteristics they possess.

6. Discuss the financial assistance available to a small business

OPENING VIGNETTE: DOLL MAKER DISARMED BY SUCCESS

The Georgetown Collection Inc.(doll manufactures) was getting ready for the Christmas season with a collectable doll accompanied by an illustrated novel that tells the doll's own story. They had competition but had a major pricing advantage over them of $23.

They ordered and received 40,000 dolls from China only to find that their arms fell off when played with. One hundred employees worked over-time, late into the night fixing the arms, making them ready to be sold. The over-time expense used up most of the capital they needed for a financial safety net. The demand for these dolls became so great they had to invest additional funds to expand both their telephone ordering system as well as their order-filling system.

Order takers were difficult to get since L.L.Bean was nearby and was using the available supply of experienced order takers. They had to learn how to take advantage of ways to manage their success, achieve enough sales to survive and face the obstacles associated with rapid expansion. They experienced the same serious problems including production, warehousing, distribution, staffing, sales and competitive pressures that are responsible for many small companies failures.

This vignette points out that small companies must plan for success as well as near failures. It calls for careful planning and managing of resources and the ability to make supplementary plans that can take care of an emergency.

KEY TERMS

Small Business Administration (SBA) - Federal agency charged with assisting small businesses.

Small business - Independently owned and managed business that does not dominate its market.

Entrepreneur - Businessperson who accepts both the risks and the opportunities involved in creating and operating a new business venture.

Minority Enterprise Small Business Investment Company (MESBIC) - Federally sponsored company that specializes in financing minority-owned and -operated businesses.

Guaranteed loans program - Program in which the SBA guarantees to repay 75-85 percent of small business commercial loans up to $750,000.

Immediate participation loans program - Program in which small businesses are loaned funds put up jointly by banks and the SBA

Local development companies (LCDs) program - Program in which the SBA works with local for-profit or nonprofit organizations seeking to boost a communities economy.

Management consultant - Independent outside specialist hired to help managers solve business problems.

Service Corps of Retired Executives (SCORE) - SBA program in which retired executives work with small businesses on a volunteer basis.

Active Corps of Executives (ACE) - SBA program in which currently employed executives work with small businesses on a volunteer basis.

Small Business Institute (SBI) - SBA program in which college and university students and instructors work with small businesspeople to help solve specific problems.

Small Business Development Center (SBDC) - SBA program designed to consolidate information from various disciplines and make it available to small businesses.

Networking - Interactions among businesspeople for the purpose of discussing mutual problems and opportunities and perhaps pooling resources.

Franchise - Arrangement in which a buyer (franchisee) purchases the right to sell the good or service of the seller (franchiser).

TRUE AND FALSE QUESTIONS

1. The Small Business Administration defines small business on two factors, the number of employees and the total annual sales.

2. Statistics show that the easiest small business to get started is that of manufacturing.

51

3.   Relative to their total employment, small firms hire at twice the rate as large ones.

4.   The more resources an industry requires, the harder it is to start a business and the less likely that the industry is dominated by small firms.

5.   It has been shown that entrepreneurs rather work for themselves rather than others because they are basically afraid of hard work.

6.   "Generation Xer's" are people in their twenties and early thirties.

7.   Black-owned businesses are increasing two and one-half times faster than all other types of start-ups.

8.   On-line commerce gives small businesses a disadvantage to reach a global market.

9.   The failure rate among small businesses has been declining in recent years.

10.   There may be many reasons for small businesses to fail but neglect is not one of them.

MULTIPLE CHOICE QUESTIONS

1.   A small business:
          a. cannot be part of another business
          b. operation must be their own bosses
          c. has very little influence in its market
          d. all of the above

2.   You are most likely to find small business in:
          a. service industry
          b. retailing
          c. wholesaling
          d. all the above

3.   The largest and fastest growing segment of small business enterprises are:
          a. wholesaling
          b. retailing
          c. services
          d. manufacturing

4.   Most successful entrepreneurs have a strong desire to:
a. let others do their work
b. enjoy taking risks
c. want to work for others
d. have little creative expression

5.   More than any other industry group, manufacturing lends itself to big business because a great deal of money is need for:
a. equipment
b. energy
c. raw materials
d. all of above

6.   Generation X entrepreneurs tend to create companies that are focused on:
a. doing good as well as making money
b. fast turn-over business
c. less customer centered businesses
d. pre-packaged products

7.   While failures in small business have declined recently, almost_____firms fail each year:
a. 50,000
b. 100,000
c. 200,000
d. 300,000

8.   Almost___% of all U.S. firms with fewer than 500 employees are owned or controlled by women.
a. 25%
b. 33 1/3%
c. 45%
d. 10%

9.   The Small Business Administration says that slightly less than____% of all new businesses can expect to survive for six years.
a. 25%
b. 33 1/3%
c. 40%
d. 60%

10.   A factor typically cited to explain small business success is:
a. hard work, drive and dedication
b. market demand for the product or services provided
c. managerial competence
d. all of the above

11. An advantage of buying an existing business rather than starting from scratch is:
        a. you can nurture it to growth
        b. you can set its personality to fit yours
        c. you have an existing customer base
        d. all of the above

12. The best way to gain knowledge about a market is to:
        a. read about it
        b. go to college to learn about it
        c. work in it
        d. ask friends about it

13. A sheltered environment for new businesses that generally includes cost sharing and other subsidies is called a/an:
        a. incubator
        b. venture capitalist
        c. local development company program
        d. small business investment company plan

14. The Small Business Administration has a service for small businesses an example is:
        a. Service Corps of Retired Executive
        b. Small Business Institute
        c. Small Business Development Center
        d. all of the above

15. A person owning a McDonald's fast food restaurant is called a(n):
        a. franchiser
        b. franchisee
        c. employee
        d. trainee

ANSWERS TO TRUE AND FALLS QUESTIONS

1. True	6. True
2. False	7. True
3. True	8. False
4. True	9. True
5. False	10. False

ANSWERS TO MULTIPLE CHOICE QUESTIONS

1. D	6. A	11. C
2. D	7. B	12. C
3. C	8. B	13. A
4. B	9. C	14. D
5. D	10. D	15. B

CHAPTER 9
UNDERSTANDING EMPLOYEE MOTIVATION AND LEADERSHIP

CHAPTER OVERVIEW

The foundation of good human relations--the interaction between employers and employees and their attitudes toward one another--is a satisfied work force. Job satisfaction is the degree of enjoyment that people derive from performing their jobs. Satisfied employees are likely to have high morale and be more committed and loyal. They are more likely to work hard and make useful contributions to the organization.

Dissatisfied workers are far more likely to be absent for minor illnesses, personal reasons, or a general disinclination to go to work. Low morale may result in high turnover. U.S. workers morale and satisfaction have started to improve after several years of decline. When companies can no longer provide job security, they can assist employees in rethinking the nature of their roles in alternative organizational systems.

The most profitable companies succeed in inspiring loyalty from customers, investors, and employees. The average corporation loses half of their workforce every four years. Motivation is the set of forces that cause people to behave in a certain way. Research has shown that attention that workers receive from their managers was very motivating to the workers.

There are six major motivational theories: the human resources model, the hierarchy of needs model, the two-factor theory, the expectancy theory, equity theory and the goal-setting theory. Managers who subscribe to Theory X believe people are naturally lazy, those who believe in Theory Y feel workers are naturally ambitious. Maslow's theory states that lower level-need must be met before a person will try to satisfy those on a higher level. Herzberg's two factor theory stated that hygiene factors affect motivation and satisfaction only if they are absent or fail to meet expectations.

The expectancy theory suggests that people are motivated to work toward rewards which they want and which they believe they have a reasonable chance to obtain. Equity theory focuses on people evaluating their treatment by the organization relative to the treatment of others. Goal setting theory states that if the goal is too easy or too difficult it tends not to be motivating.

Reinforcement strategies reward people with pay, praise, promotion, and job security. Punishment is designed to change behavior by presenting people with unpleasant consequences if they fail to change in desirable ways. Management by objectives is inherently a set of procedures involving both managers and subordinates in setting goals and evaluating progress. In participative management empowered employees are given a voice in how they do their jobs and how the company is managed.

Multifunctional training programs are designed to give every employee a wide range of production skills. Additional motivating factors can be financial incentives, job enrichment and job redesign. Modified work schedules have become popular in industry where work-share and flextime programs are offered. With the advent of computers and the new technology, telecommuting and virtual offices have found favor in industry.

Leadership is the process of motivating others to work to meet specific objectives. Leadership styles differ from autocratic to democratic to free-rein, each having its own advantages and disadvantages.

CHAPTER OBJECTIVES

1. Define good human relations

2. Explain the importance of job satisfaction and morale

3. Describe recent trends in managing satisfaction and morale

4. Explain some results of high and low morale

5. Describe some contemporary motivational theories

6. Show how Maslow's theory operates in the workplace

7. Differentiate between theory X and Y

8. Describe how Management by Objective works

OPENING VIGNETTE: WHAT WOULD CAPITALISM DO WITHOUT "BOSSY BOSSES"?

In a business that is known for a high turnover of workers, the Chick-fil fast food chicken chain is different. The employee turn over rate of some fast food companies is as high as 300 percent, Chicken-fil is proud of their 50% turnover of hourly employees and only 35% for operators.

They believe a company in order to build loyalty must do right by employees and still do well. The 600 restaurants in 34 states follow what the owners believe is a "Christian ethic". They believe in a strong corporate culture of fair play and trust. Chicken-fil gives operators a good income has never laid off anyone. The company builds a store and leases it to the operator for a one time $5,000 fee and then splits the profits. A minimum income of $30,000 is guaranteed, one operator of two shops makes $100,000 annually. The company offers attractive perks and benefits. In 1996 it gave a trip to Bermuda for 400 people and their spouses, and in 1997 a trip to Orlando was the perk. Any operator increasing sales by 20 percent in one year is given a car.

Using a multifaceted approach, Chick-fil has been able to motivate its workforce so that workers not only stay on the job but perform at the highest level. The company feels that people are not purely economic animals but are political, psychological beings as well. Material, social and emotional needs and desires must be met to motivate workers. Chicken-fil treats their workers right and gets loyalty in return.

KEY TERMS

Human relations - Interactions between employers and employees and their attitudes toward one another.

Job satisfaction - Degree of enjoyment that people derive from performing their jobs.

Morale - Overall attitude that employees have toward their workplace.

Motivation - The set of forces that cause people to behave in certain ways.

Classical theory of motivation - Theory that workers are motivated solely by money.

Hawthorne effect - Tendency for productivity to increase when workers believe they are receiving special attention from management.

Theory X - Theory of motivation holding that people are naturally irresponsible and uncooperative.

Theory Y - Theory of motivation holding that people are naturally responsible, growth-orientated, self-motivated, and interested in being productive.

Hierarchy of human needs model - Theory of motivation describing five levels of human needs and arguing that basic needs must be fulfilled before people work to satisfy higher-level needs.

Two-factor theory - Theory of motivation holding that job satisfaction depends on two types of factors, hygiene and motivation.

Expectancy theory - Theory of motivation holding that people are motivated to work toward rewards that they want and that they believe they have a reasonable chance of obtaining.

Equity theory - Theory of motivation holding that people evaluate their treatment by employers relative to the treatment of others.

Reinforcement - Theory that behavior can be encouraged or discouraged by means of rewards or punishments.

Management by objective (MBO) - Set of procedures involving both managers and subordinates in setting goals and evaluating progress.

Participative management and empowerment - Method of increasing job satisfaction by giving employees a voice in the management of their jobs and the company.

Job enrichment - Method of increasing job satisfaction by adding one or more motivating factors to job activities.

Job redesigns - Method of increasing job satisfaction by designing a more satisfactory fit between workers and their jobs.

Work sharing (or Job sharing) - Method of increasing job satisfaction by allowing two or more people to share a single full-time job.

Flextime programs - Method of increasing job satisfaction by allowing workers to adjust work schedules on a daily or weekly basis.

Telecommuting - Form of flextime that allows people to perform some or all of a job away from standard office settings.

Leadership - Process of motivating others to work to meet specific objectives.

Managerial style - Pattern of behavior that a manager exhibits in dealing with subordinates.

Autocratic style - Managerial style in which managers generally issue orders and expect them to be obeyed without question.

Democratic style - Managerial style in which managers generally ask for input from subordinates but retain final decision-making power.

Free-rein style - Managerial style in which managers typically serve as advisors to subordinates who are allowed to make decisions.

Contingency approach - Approach to managerial style holding that the appropriate behavior in any situation is dependent (contingent) on the unique elements of that situation.

TRUE AND FALSE QUESTIONS

1. Workers grievances, absence from the job, high worker turn over is a sign of poor morale.

2. U.S. workers morale was deemed high when compared to that of Canadian, British and German workers.

3. The average public corporation loses half of its workforce every four years.

4. Workers are motivated solely by money.

5. The Hawthorne Study showed that workers increased productivity when they were receiving attention from management.

6. McGregor's Theory Y states that managers following this theory feel that workers are naturally lazy and uncooperative and must therefore be punished or rewarded to be made productive.

7. Maslow's Hierarchy of Needs model proposes that security is the first step needed to be achieved in order to climb the ladder of needs.

8. In goal-setting theory goals that are too easy or too difficult fail to motivate workers.

9. Management by objectives is inherently a set of procedures involving both managers and subordinates in setting goals and evaluating progress.

10. Profit sharing can be explained as, "In good times everyone gets a piece of the pie; in bad times, all have to buckle down".

MULTIPLE CHOICE QUESTIONS

1. Workers have needs and desires, they want recognition in:
   - a. material payment
   - b. social recognition
   - c. emotional satisfaction
   - d. all of the above

2. Employees make useful contributions to the organization and have fewer grievances when they:
   - a. belong to a union
   - b. have high morale
   - c. travel to work in less than 30 minutes
   - d. all the above

3. Survey results suggest that satisfaction and morale of U.S. employees have:
   - a. declined
   - b. improved
   - c. remain the same
   - d. is not able to be measured

4. When employees feel secure in their jobs the reaction is:
   - a. a slow down in production
   - b. more fun, less work on the job
   - c. production rate rises
   - d. none of the above

5. According to the so-called **classical** theory of motivation workers are motivated solely by:
   - a. money
   - b. fear
   - c. unionization
   - d. conditions of the workplace

6. Scientific management is concerned with:
   - a. time-and-motion studies
   - b. job duty breakdown
   - c. efficient tools and machinery
   - d. all of the above

7. McGregor's Theory Y states that:
   - a. physiological needs come first
   - b. employees must be pushed to perform
   - c. employees have a natural tendency to cooperate
   - d. different people have different needs

8.	The two-factor theory deals with hygiene factors that affect motivation and satisfaction only they are absent or fail to meet expectations. The hygiene factors are the work of:
	a. Maslow
	b. Herzberg
	c. McGregor
	d. Taylor

9.	Maslow said that the need to grow and develop one's capabilities and to achieve new and meaningful goals are called:
	a. self-actualization
	b. esteem needs
	c. social needs
	d. none of the above

10.	The focus on social comparisons, people evaluating their treatment by the organization relative to the treatment of others is the theory called:
	a. expectancy
	b. equity
	c. behavior
	d. goal-setting

11.	Studies show that rewards are more likely than punishments to motivate and increase job satisfaction. They usually work only if employees:
	a. believe that they can actually perform better by making an effort
	b. believe that they will, in fact, receive rewards for performing better
	c. want the reward that the company has to offer
	d. all of the above

12.	One major disadvantage of Management by Objective is that:
	a. it takes time to implement at every level of the organization
	b. it means multiple conferences with the employee
	c. not everyone can figure out an objective
	d. none of the above

13.	Team management is not for everyone because:
	a. many people will be frustrated by responsibilities that they are not equipped to handle
	b. some workers see the invitation to participate as more symbolic than substantive
	c. some feel that the commitment from top management is not there
	d. all of the above

14.   Job-enrichment programs are designed to add more motivating factors to the job activities such as:

        a. job rotation

        b. increasing responsibilities

        c. giving more control over their own scheduling

        d. all of the above

15,   The managerial style that generally issues orders and expects them to be obeyed without question is called:

        a. democratic

        b. free-rein

        c. autocratic

        d. none of the above

ANSWERS TO TRUE AND FALSE QUESTIONS

1. True	6. False
2. True	7. False
3. True	8. True
4. False	9. True
5. True	10. True

ANSWERS TO MULTIPLE CHOICE QUESTIONS

1. D	6. D	11. D
2. B	7. C	12. A
3. B	8. B	13. D
4. C	9. A	14. D
5. A	10. B	15. C

CHAPTER 10
MANAGING HUMAN RESOURCES AND LABOR RELATIONS

CHAPTER OVERVIEW

Human resource management is the development and administration of programs to enhance the quality and performance of people working in an organization. The human resource manager, sometimes called the personnel manager, is involved in recruiting, training, and developing employees. This individual sets up evaluation, compensation and benefits programs for the workers.

All employment decisions are based on job relatedness and the matching of persons to the job. Human resource planning starts with job analyses, job description and job specification. The next task is forecasting the needs and then staffing the organization. Both external and internal staffing is used.

Most steps start with recruitment, selection of applicants, studying the resume and screening interviewees. Many organizations give ability and aptitude tests. Many companies insist on physical exams before hiring. When hiring from within, closed promotion and open promotion systems are used. Seniority many times is taken into consideration before making promotional decisions.

New workers are given an orientation, explaining the new job and then trained on-the-job, off-the-job and vestibule training which is training under simulated conditions.

Since many of the baby boomers are retiring, a steady supply of new workers will be needed. Many will be minority workers, immigrants and others who will need training. Apprentice programs are becoming popular starting at some vocational schools.

All workers performances are evaluated. Some informally by passing remarks such as "you are doing OK", others have formal written evaluations of the worker. Written appraisals are especially necessary for disciplinary action such as demotions and terminations.

Compensation systems are set up to include wages, salaries, and benefits. Organizations have special pay programs designed to motivate high performance. Sales personnel receive bonuses for selling above quotas and others may receive merit salary raises for high performances. Executives commonly receive stock options.

As the range of benefits grows so has the concern for containing their costs. The so-called cafeteria benefit plan gives workers a choice of what benefits they particularly want. They may choose a bigger cut in health costs, more money for retirement, or other options to fit their needs.

Human resource managers are confronted by a number of legal issues: equal employment opportunity, equal pay and comparable worth, occupation safety and health and the doctrine of employment-at-will. The U.S. government has passed laws concerning these issues that protect the workers from various types of harassment and unfair hiring practices.

Cutbacks and downsizing are related trends in business today. Human resource managers face a number of ongoing challenges in their efforts to keep their organization staffed with effective work forces. Work force diversity is a challenge that is concerned with the range of workers' attitudes, values, beliefs, and behaviors that differ by gender, race and ethnicity. Age and physical abilities also must be considered. Diversity training-programs are used to improve employees' awareness of differences in attitudes and behavior patterns among co-workers.

Labor unions were organized to protect workers from unfair labor practices. Collective bargaining is the process by which union leaders and managers negotiate conditions of employment.
Labor unions have been in decline in the last 40 years. Many reasons are given for the decline, workers earn more money today, anti-unionization strategies by corporations and the inability of unions to prevent give-backs. Labor and management in some industries are beginning to favor contracts that establish formal mechanisms for greater worker input into management decisions.

Major labor laws were enacted between 1932 and 1959. These laws dealt with specific groups and specific issues. Some of these laws were passed to help the union movement progress, while others were passed to restrict certain workers rights.

When the process of collective bargaining fails the result may be a strike (picketing and boycotts) or a lockout (hiring of strike breakers), Both activities stop the wheels of production for an organization. Mediation, voluntary arbitration and compulsory arbitration are sometimes used to settle disputes.

CHAPTER OBJECTIVES

1. Explain how human resource managers plan for staffing an organization.

2. Identify how collective bargaining works

3. Describe the five basic principles that underlie human resource policies in the U.S.

4. Identify the major laws governing labor-management relations.

5. Explain the results when collective bargaining fails to reach an agreement.

6. Differentiate between mediation, voluntary arbitration and compulsory arbitration.

OPENING VIGNETTE: MARRIOTT CLEARS A PATHWAY TO PRODUCTIVE EMPLOYMENT

When President Clinton signed legislation requiring millions of welfare recipients to find work he asked private industry to help find jobs for these people. Marriott organized a program called Pathways to Independence and enrolled nearly 600 people at their hotels in 15 cities.

Pathways teaches people with little or no work experience skills how to hold a job. They learn everything from personal hygiene to punctuality. They learn to talk out conflicts rather than fight, how to use checking accounts and handle money.

With government assistance the program costs Marriott $2,300 per trainee. Graduates have a 13-percent turnover on these jobs compared to 37-percent for average workers. Seventy five percent stay with the company more than 300 days.

This program relates what private industry can do for the unfortunate, untrained people on welfare to get and hold jobs. It also indicates that a program such as this one makes bottom-line sense and as the chairman of the board at Marriott explained, it is good business as well as the right thing to do.

KEY TERMS

Human resource management - Development and administration of programs to enhance the quality and performance of a company's work force.

Human resource managers - Managers responsible for hiring, training, evaluating, and compensating employees.

Job relatedness - Principle that all employment decisions should be based on the requirements of the jobs in question.

Person-job matching - Process of matching the right person to the right job.

Job analysis - Evaluation of the duties and qualities required by a job.

Job description - Outline of the objectives, tasks, and responsibilities of a job.

Job specification - Description of the skills, education, and experience required by a job.

Closed promotion system - System by which managers decide, often informally, which workers are considered for promotions.

Open promotion system - System by which employees apply, test, and interview for available jobs, requirements of which are posted.

On-the-job training - Training, sometimes informal, conducted while an employee is at work.

Off-the-job training - Training conducted in a controlled environment away from the work site.

Vestibule training - Off-the-job training conducted in a simulated environment.

Performance appraisal - Evaluation, often in writing, of an employee's job performance.

Compensation system - Total package offered by a company to employees in return for their labor.

Wages - Compensation in the form of money paid for time worked.

Salary - Compensation in the form of money paid for discharging the responsibilities of a job.

Incentive program - Special compensation program designed to motivate high performance.

Bonus - Individual performance incentive in the form of a special payment made over and above the employee's salary.

Merit salary system - Incentive program linking compensation to performance in nonsales jobs.

Pay-for-performance (or **Variable pay**) - Individual incentive that rewards a manger for especially productive output.

Profit-sharing plan - Incentive program for distributing bonuses to employees for company profits above a certain level.

Gain-sharing plan - Incentive program for distributing bonuses to employees whose performances improve productivity.

Pay-for-knowledge plan - Incentive program to encourage employees to learn new skills or become proficient at different jobs.

Benefits - Compensation other than wages and salaries.

Worker's compensation insurance - Legally required insurance for compensating workers injured on the job.

Cafeteria benefits plan - Benefits plan that establishes dollar amount of benefits per employee and allows employees to choose from a variety of alternative benefits.

Equal employment opportunity - Legally mandated nondiscrimination in employment on the basis of race, creed, sex, or national origin.

Affirmative action program - Legally mandated program for recruiting qualified employees belonging to racial, gender, or ethnic groups that are underrepresented in an organization.

Reverse discrimination - Practice of discriminating against well-represented groups by overhiring members of underrepresented groups.

Comparable worth - Principle that women should receive the same pay for traditionally "female" jobs of the same worth to a company as traditionally "male" job.

Occupational Safety and Health Administration (OSHA) - Federal agency that sets and enforces guidelines for protecting workers from unsafe conditions and potential health hazards in the workplace.

Work force diversity - Range of workers' attitudes, values, and behaviors that differ by gender, race, and ethnicity.

Diversity training - Programs designed to improve employee awareness of differences in attitudes and behaviors of co-workers from different racial, ethnic, or gender group.

Contingent worker - Temporary employee hired to supplement an organization's permanent work force.

Labor union - Group of individuals working together formally to achieve shared job-related goals.

Collective bargaining - Process by which labor and management negotiate conditions of employment for workers represented by the union.

Norris-LaGuardia Act (1932) - Federal law limiting the ability of courts to issue injunctions prohibiting certain union activities.

National Labor Relations Act (Wagner Act) (1935) - Federal law protecting the rights of workers to form unions, bargain collectively, and engage in strikes to achieve their goals.

National Labor Relations Board (NLRB) - Federal agency established by the National Labor Relations Act to enforce its provisions.

Fair Labor Standards Act (1938) - Federal law setting minimum wage and maximum number of hours in the workweek.

Labor-Management Relations Act (Taft-Hatley Act) (1947) - Federal law defining certain union practices as unfair and illegal.

Closed shop - Work place in which an employer may hire only workers already belonging to a union.

Labor-Management Reporting and Disclosure Act (Landrum-Griffin Act) (1959) - Federal law imposing regulations on internal unions procedures, including elections of national leaders and filing of financial-disclosure statements.

Strike - Labor action in which employees temporarily walk off the job and refuse to work.

Economic strike - Strike usually triggered by stalemate over one or more mandatory bargaining items.

Picketing - Labor action in which workers publicize their grievances at the entrance to an employer's facility.

Boycott - Labor action in which workers refuse to buy the products of a targeted employer.

Lockout - Management tactic whereby workers are denied access to their workplace.

Strikebreaker - Worker hired as permanent or temporary replacement for a striking employee.

Mediation - Method of resolving a labor dispute in which a third party advises on, but does not impose, a settlement.

Voluntary arbitration - Method of resolving a labor dispute in which both parties agree to submit to the judgment of a neutral party.

Compulsory arbitration - Method of resolving a labor dispute in which both parties are legally required to accept the judgment of a neutral party.

TRUE AND FALSE QUESTIONS

1. The term human resource management is interchangeable with the title personnel manager.

2. Job analysis is a statement outlining the objectives, tasks, and responsibilities of a job.

3. Job specifications is the evaluation of duties required by a particular job.

4. In closed promotion systems, mangers decide which workers will be considered for promotion.

5. Vestibule training takes place at the sight the worker will be working in the future.

6. Performance appraisals are designed to show more precisely how well workers are doing their jobs.

7. Wages are paid for discharging the responsibilities of a job while salaries are paid for time worked.

8.   Sales people tend to get bonuses and non-sales people get merit salary raises.

9.   About 60 percent of U.S. workers are covered by pension plans of some kind.

10.   Under the Equal Employment Opportunity Act of 1992, the EEOC cannot file civil suits in federal court on behalf of individuals who claim that their rights have been violated.

MULTIPLE CHOICE QUESTIONS

1.   The Equal Employment Opportunity Act of 1992 is concerned with discrimination as it is used against:
        a. race
        b. color
        c. sex
        d. all of the above

2.   The decision not to hire someone because the person is 65 years old would be prosecuted under the category of:
        a. Equal employment opportunity
        b. equal pay
        c. comparable worth
        d. occupational safety and health

3.   Sexual harassment is a form of employer or management behavior that falls under the category of employment discrimination and is prohibited by:
        a. Equal Opportunity Act
        b. Affirmative Action
        c. Reverse Discrimination laws
        d. all of the above

4.   There seems to be an invisible but very real barrier over their heads that keeps women and minorities from advancing to higher levels in U.S. organizations. This is termed:
        a. doctrine of employment-at-will
        b. glass ceiling
        c. comparative worth
        d. none of the above

5.   OSHA deals with:
        a. age discrimination
        b. sexual discrimination
        c. unsafe working conditions
        d. protecting workers from being fired

6. Work force diversity deals with workers:
   a. beliefs
   b. ages
   c. ethnicity
   d. all of the above

7. Contingent workers are employees hired to:
   a. work as skilled professionals
   b. supplement a permanent work force
   c. supervise on-line production
   d. none of the above

8. Workers usually unionize because:
   a. other industries have unions
   b. management insists upon it
   c. they feel conditions are bad
   d. it is the social thing to do

9. Union membership in the U.S. for wage and salary employees are about_____of the working force:
   a. 20%
   b. 26%
   c. 45%
   d. 57%

10 A factor in declining union power is:
   a. composition of the workforce
   b. anti-unionization strategies
   c. negotiated concessions
   d. all of the above

11. The act that persuaded lawmakers that the legal environment discriminated against the collective efforts of workers to improve working conditions was:
   a. Norris-LaGuardia Act
   b. Wagner Act
   c. Fair Labor Standards Act
   d. none of the above

12. The act that put labor unions on a more equal footing with management in terms of the rights of employees to organize and bargain was:
   a. Norris-LaGuardia Act
   b. National Labor Relations Act
   c. Fair Labor Standards Act
   d. none of the above

13. The Taft-Hartley Act:
   a. prohibited featherbedding
   b. prohibited closed shop
   c. allowed states to enact right-to-work laws
   d. all of the above

14. The Landrum-Griffin Act :
   a. required the election of national union leaders once every five years
   b. set the rule any work over 40 hours must be paid at time and a half scale
   c. permitted for the first time collective bargaining among workers.
   d. set up a mandatory cooling off period

15. When employers deny employees access to the workplace it is called a:
   a. strike
   b. boycott
   c. lockout
   d. picketing

ANSWERS TO TRUE AND FALSE QUESTIONS

1. True	6. True
2. False	7. False
3. False	8. True
4. True	9. True
5. False	10. False

ANSWERS TO MULTIPLE CHOICE QUESTIONS

1. D	6. D	11. A
2. A	7. B	12. B
3. A	8. C	13. D
4. B	9. B	14. A
5. C	10. D	15. C

CHAPTER 11
MANAGING PRODUCTION AND IMPROVING QUALITY

CHAPTER OVERVIEW

Production, formerly concerned with goods, is now equally concerned with services. In 1995, employment in service industries accounted for almost 80% of the total U.S. work force. Services will remain the faster-growing employment source in the immediate future. All business provides services, even if their primary concern is the manufacturing of goods.

Production provides consumers with many utilities: time, place, ownership-possession, and form. The term production has been replaced by the term operations. Operation processes are characterized in two ways: transformation technology and by the analytic or synthetic nature of the process during transformation. Transformation technology deals with the following processes: chemical, fabrication, assembly, transport and clerical.

High contact services, deal directly with the customer (i.e.: a barbershop) and must be more concerned with the cleanliness and appearance of the "shop" than the low-contact services. Low contact services such as a mail order firm, need not concern themselves with these problems since customers are not directly involved where the service is performed. Often services are intangible, cannot be touched, tasted, smelled or seen (i.e.: dry cleaning service).

There are five major categories in key planning of operations: capacity, location, layout, quality and methods. A master production schedule shows which products will be produced, when production will occur, and what resources will be used during specified time periods. Operations control requires managers to monitor production performance with materials management as well as controlling the production process. Materials management focuses on product design and standardization as well as transportation, warehousing and purchasing.

Inventory control is an important part of operations It is the receiving, storing, handling and counting of all raw materials, partly finished goods, and finished goods in the organization's possession. A number of tools used in controlling operations are the just-in-time system, material requirements planning, quality control and worker training. Companies that compare their systems and products to that of their competitors must adjust their techniques and up-date their business practices if they want to stay competitive

CHAPTER OBJECTIVES

1. Identify the three ways of classifying operation processes.

2. Explain the differences between service operations and goods production.

3. Explain the five forms of transformation technology in manufacturing.

4. Describe the differences between the analytic and synthetic processes in manufacturing.

5. Identify the five major planning activity categories.

6. Explain the activities necessary in Total Quality Management (TIM).

OPENING VIGNETTE: CRAFTY BREWERS WITH A MARKETING ANGLE

Large beer brewers are getting annoyed with the smaller brewers for advertising that they take painstaking care making beer in small batches. They claim that the large brewers mass produced their beer using less care. Only 10% of the specialty brewers actually brew their own beer. They are known as contract brewers because they give large breweries a recipe and a contract asking them to make the beer for them. Anheuser Busch says these small companies are duping consumers. The smaller companies disagree stating that they give their own specifications to the large companies and all they have to do is make the beer to these specification. They do not consider this duping the consumer.

Specialty brewers sales soared by 50% last year, while industry wide sales of beer have been flat. Large companies feel that the success has come because of marketing methods rather than superior production methods or a quality breakthrough. The smaller breweries have changed their story, now they say it is "crafted with care". This is an example of a low contact business, the customer really does not know what goes on in the production end of the brewery.

KEY TERMS

Service operations - Business activities that provide tangible and intangible services.
Goods production - Business operations that create tangible products.
Utility - A product's ability to satisfy a human want.
Operations (or **Production**) **management** - Systematic direction and control of the processes that transform resources into finished products.
Operations managers - Managers responsible for production, inventory, and quality control.
Operations process - Set of methods and technologies used in the production of a good or service.
High-contact system - Level of service-customer contact in which the customer receives the service as part of the system.

Low-contact system - Level of service-customer contact in which the customer need not be a part of the system to receive the service.

Capacity - Amount of a product that a company can produce under normal working conditions.

Process layout - Spatial arrangement of production activities that groups equipment and people according to function.

Product layout - Spatial arrangement of production activities designed to move resources through a smooth, fixed sequence of steps.

Assembly line - Product layout in which a product moves step-by-step through a plant on conveyor belts and other equipment until it is completed.

Cellular layout - Spatial arrangement of production facilities designed to move families of products through similar flow paths.

Quality - A product's fitness for use; its success in offering features that consumers want.

Operations control - Process of monitoring production performance by comparing results with plans.

Materials management - Planning, organizing, and controlling the flow of materials from design through distribution of finished goods.

Standardization - Use, where possible, of standard and uniform components in the production process.

Inventory control - Receiving, storing, handling, and counting of all raw materials, partly finished goods and finished goods.

Just-in-time (JIT) production system - Production method that brings together all materials and parts needed at each production stage at the precise moment at which they are required.

Material requirements planning (MRP) - Production control method in which a bill of materials is used to ensure that the right amounts of materials are delivered to the right place at the right time.

Quality control - Management of the production process designed to manufacture goods or supply services that meet specific quality standards.

Quality improvement team (or **Quality circle**) - TQM tool in which groups of work employees work together as a team to improve quality.

Total quality management (TQM) (or **Quality assurance**) - The sum of all activities involved in getting quality products into the marketplace.

Performance quality - The performance features offered by a product.

Quality reliability - Consistency of a product's quality from unit to unit.

Quality ownership - Principle of total quality management that holds that quality belongs to each person who creates it while performing a job.

Competitive product analysis - Process by which a company analyzes a competitor's products to identify desirable improvements in its own.

Statistical process control (SPC) - Evaluation methods that allow managers to analyze variations in a company's production activities.

Control chart - Process control method that plots test sampling results on a diagram to determine when a process is beginning to depart from normal operating conditions.

Quality/cost study - Method of improving quality by identifying current costs and areas with the greatest cost-saving potential.

TRUE AND FALSE QUESTIONS

T   1.   The concept of production is now concerned as much with services as it is with goods.

F   2.   Although production in the U.S. has grown 50% the services industry has remained flat.

T   3.   Products provide customers with many utilities.

F   4.   Place utility is when a company turns out ornaments in time for Christmas.

T   5.   An operations process is the set of methods and technologies used in the production of a good or a service.

T   6.   The fabrication processes mechanically alters the basic shape or form of a product.

T   7.   Services must focus on both the transformation process and its outcome. Pizza makers thus have to be concerned with the pizza and on delivering it to the buyer.

F   8.   Capacity planning means ensuring that a firms production strictly adheres to and not exceed the normal demand for its product.

F   9.   In planning high-contact services, companies have some options: services may be located near or far from shopping areas.

T   10. Cellular layouts are used when families of products can follow similar flow paths.

MULTIPLE CHOICE QUESTIONS

1.   The service sector in 1995 provided nearly____% of national income:
     a. 20%
     b. 40%
     c. 50%
     d. 60%

2.   By turning raw materials into finished goods, production creates:
     a. time utility
     b. place utility
     c. ownership utility
     d. form utility

3. By making Christmas trees available in early December the company is creating:
    a. form utility
    b. ownership utility
    c. time utility
    d. place utility

4. The fabrication process of transformation technology:
    a. mechanically alters the basic shape or form of a product.
    b. chemically alters raw materials
    c. puts together various components
    d. combines data on machine breakdowns in production

5. The analytic process:
    a. reduces incoming goods to packaged parts
    b. combines raw materials to produce a finished product
    c. plays an important part in package design
    d. none of the above

6. An example of a high contact system is:
    a. Shopper's TV Channel Service
    b. Lands End Catalog Service
    c. Sacks Fifth Avenue Service
    d. L.L. Bean Service

7. Intangible service is offered by:
    a. lawyers
    b. hardware stores
    c. ice cream parlors
    d. carpenters

8. An example of a high degree of unstorability is:
    a. lumber
    b. transportation
    c. ready-to-wear
    d. fashion dresses

9. High-contact services:
    a. has no restrictions
    b. must locate near customers
    c. must locate near raw materials
    d. has capital restrictions

10. Today's business strategy is to:
    a. open a shop and ask people to come to you
    b. find where people already are and bring your product to them
    c. choose a site and advertise heavily
    d. locate in a low rent district

11. Layout planning targets requirements of:
    a. the product
    b. the equipment
    c. the employees
    d. all of above

12. A master production schedule shows:
    a. which products will be produced
    b. when production will occur
    c. what resources will be used
    d. all of the above

13. The one area that is not included in material management is:
    a. advertising
    b. transportation
    c. warehousing
    d. purchasing

14. The one area not included in inventory control is:
    a. receiving
    b. storing
    c. handling
    d. ticketing

15. Quality costs are associated with_____defective goods and services:
    a. making
    b. repairing
    c. preventing
    d. all of the above

ANSWERS TO TRUE AND FALSE QUESTIONS

1. True
2. False
3. True
4. False
5. True

6. True
7. True
8. False
9. False
10. True

ANSWERS TO MULTIPLE CHOICE QUESTIONS

1. D
2. D
3. C
4. A
5. A

6. C
7. A
8. B
9. B
10. B

11. D
12. D
13. A
14. D
15. D

CHAPTER 12
UNDERSTANDING ACCOUNTING AND INFORMATION SYSTEMS

CHAPTER OVERVIEW

Accounting is a comprehensive system for collecting, analyzing, and communicating financial information. The system is an organized procedure for identifying, measuring, recording, and retaining financial information so that it can be used in accounting statements and management reports. The controller, who heads up the accounting system, manages all the firm's accounting. Bookkeeping plays a part by recording the accounting transactions.

Financial accounting focuses on the activities of the company as a whole rather than individual departments or divisions. Managerial accounting serves internal users such as departments, projects, etc. It is used by managers to make decisions for their departments. Certified public accountants offer accounting services to the public and are licensed by the state. They do auditing and tax services for clients.

All accountants rely on record keeping to enter and track business transactions. As initial records are received, they are sorted and entered in a journal. These records are summarized in a final record called the ledger. At the end of the year, all accounts in the ledger are totaled, and the firm's financial status is assessed. Accountants have a number of equations to balance the data in journals and ledgers.

T-accounts and the double-entry system provide an important method of accounting control. Financial statements such as balance sheets, profit and loss statements, tell the accountant how a particular company is doing. Computers today speed up processing of the records and assist in producing error-free calculations.

Office automation includes the use of fax machines, voice mail and E-mail all of which have made the office more efficient. The success of the Internet (public use) has given birth to the intranet (private networks). The modern information systems have made accounting, record keeping and related work more effective and efficient.

CHAPTER OBJECTIVES

1.   Explain the differences between the duties of an accountant and a bookkeeper

2.   Describe the three concepts used in record keeping.

3.   Explain the differences between an accountant and a certified public accountant.

4.   Describe two important financial statements and explain how they reflect the financial condition of a business.

5.   Explain the use of the three financial statement ratios.

6.   Describe how double entry bookkeeping helps prevent errors in bookkeeping.

7.   Explain how computers have revolutionized information systems management.

8.   Describe the work of the multimedia communications systems.

OPENING VIGNETTE: THERE'S NO BUSINESS LIKE SHOW BUSINESS

Experience has proven that anyone with a "net profit" agreement with a movie studio will find it difficult to earn any profit at all. This sounds strange but so are the Hollywood accounting procedures. They treat advertising expenses as assets and can add to a film's expense millions in studio "overhead" charges. They also can add millions more in start-up charges from unrelated failed projects. If they believe that the movie will bring in profits for twenty years from other than U.S. theater sources, they can take 20 years to subtract the film's costs from its books.

Studios insist that the first year's box office receipts could never cover the average cost of making a movie. They only get 40% of the receipts, the movie house gets 60%. The unique accounting system makes it extremely difficult for people with so-called "net profit" interest in a movie to make any money from the interest earned. Thus even though the blockbuster hit Forrest Gump grossed approximately $650 million, it has paid no money to anyone with a net-profit interest in the film.

This vignette makes it clear that it is wise to have an accountant advise you on financial intricacies of any deals that are offered. One must be alert to "imaginative accounting" as well as to special accounting for special businesses.

KEY TERMS

Accounting - Comprehensive system for collecting, analyzing, and communicating financial information.

Bookkeeping - The recording of accounting transactions.

Accounting system - Organized means by which financial information is identified, measured, recorded, and retained for use in accounting statements and management reports.

Financial accounting system - Field of accounting concerned with external users of a company's financial information.

Managerial (or Management) accounting - Field of accounting that serves internal users of a company's financial information.

Certified Public Accountant (CPA) - Accountant licensed by the state and offering services to the public.

Audit - Systematic examination of a company's accounting system to determine whether its financial reports fairly present its operations.

Generally accepted accounting principles (GAAP) - Accepted rules and procedures governing the content and form of financial reports.

Journal - Chronological record of a firm's financial transactions, including a brief description of each.

Ledger - Record, divided into accounts and usually compiled on a monthly basis, containing summaries of all journal transactions.

Fiscal year - Twelve-month period designated for annual financial reporting purposes.

Asset - Any economic resource expected to benefit a firm or individual who owns it.

Liability - Debt owed by a firm to an outside organization or individual.

Owner's equity - Amount of money owners would receive if they sold all of a firm's assets and paid all of its liabilities.

Double-entry accounting system - Bookkeeping system that balances the accounting equation by recording the dual effects of every financial transaction.

T-account - Bookkeeping format for recording transactions that takes the shape of a *T* whose vertical line divides the account into debits (left side) and credits (right side).

Debit - Bookkeeping entry in a T-account that records increases in assets.

Credit - Bookkeeping entry in a T-account that records decreases in assets.

Financial statement - Any of several types of reports summarizing a company's financial status to aid in managerial decision making.

Balance sheet - Financial statement detailing a firm's assets, liabilities, and owner's equity.

Current asset - Asset that can be converted into cash within the following year.

Liquidity - Ease with which an asset can be converted into cash.

Accounts receivable - Amount due from a customer who has purchased goods on credit.

Merchandise inventory - Cost of merchandise that has been acquired for sale to customers and that is still on hand.

Prepaid expense - Expense, such as prepaid rent, that is paid before the upcoming period in which it is due.

Fixed asset - Asset with long-term use or value, such as land, buildings, and equipment.

Depreciation - Process of distributing the cost of an asset over its life.

Intangible asset - Nonphysical asset, such as a patent or trademark, that has economic value in the form of expected benefit.

Goodwill - Amount paid for an existing business above the value of its other assets.

Current liability - Debt that must be paid within the year.

Accounts payable - Current liabilities consisting of bills owed to suppliers, plus wages and taxes due within the upcoming year.

Long-term liability - Debt that is not due for at least a year.

Paid-in capital - Additional money, above proceeds from stock sale, paid directly to a firm by its owners.

Retained earnings - Earnings retained by a firm for its use rather than paid as dividends.

Income statement (or Profit-and-loss statement) - Financial statement listing a firm's annual revenues, expenses, and profit or loss.

Revenues - Funds that flow into a business from the sale of goods or services.

Cost of goods sold - Total cost of obtaining materials for making the products sold by a firm during the year.

Gross profit (or Gross margin) - Revenues from goods sold minus the cost of goods sold.

Operating expenses - Costs, other than the cost of goods sold, incurred in producing a good or service.

Operating income - Gross profit minus operating expenses.

Net income (or Net profit or Net earnings) - Gross profit minus operating expenses and income taxes.

Solvency ratio - Financial ratio, both short- and long-term, for estimating the risk investing in a firm.

Profitability ratio - Financial ratio fro measuring a firm's potential earnings.

Activity ratio - Financial ratio for evaluating management's use of a firm's assets.

Liquidity ratio - Solvency ratio measuring a firm's ability to pay its immediate debts.

Current ratio - Solvency ratio that determines a firm's creditworthiness by measuring its ability to pay current liabilities.

Debt ratio - Solvency ratio measuring a firm's ability to meet its long-term debts.

Debt-to-owners' equity ratio (or debt-to-equity ratio) - Solvency ration describing the extent to which a firm is financed through borrowing.

debt - A firm's total liabilities.

Return on investment (or return on equity) - Profitability ration measuring income earned for each dollar invested.

Earnings per share - Profitability ratio measuring the size of the dividend that a firm can pay shareholders.

Inventory turnover ratio - Activity ratio measuring the average number of times that inventory is sold and restocked during the year.

Information managers - Managers responsible for designing and implementing systems to gather, organize, and distribute information.

Data - Raw facts and figures

Information - The useful interpretation of data

Management information system (MIS) - System for transforming data into information that can be used in decision making.

Database - Centralized, organized collection of related data

Batch processing - Method of collecting data over a period of time and then computer processing them as a group or batch.

Real-time (or On-line) processing - Method of entering data and computer processing them immediately.

Word-processing program - Application program that allows computers to store, edit, and print letters and numbers for documents created by users.

Electronic spreadsheet - Application program with a row-and-column format that allows users to compare the effect of changes from one category to another.

Database management program - Application program for creating, storing, searching, and manipulating an organized collection of data.

Computer graphics program - Application program that converts numeric and character data into pictorial information, such as graphs and charts.

Desktop publishing - Process of combining word-processing and graphics capability to produce typeset-quality text from personal computers.

Artificial intelligence (AI) - Construction and programming of computers to imitate human thought processes.

Expert system - Form of artificial intelligence that attempts to imitate the behavior of human experts in a particular field.

Fax machine - Machine that can transmit copies of documents over telephone lines.

Voice mail - Computer-based system for receiving and delivering incoming telephone calls.

Electronic mail (E-mail) - Computer system that electronically transmits information between computers.

Data communications network - Global network (such as the Internet) that permits users to send electronic messages and information quickly and economically.

Internet - Global data communications network serving thousands of computers with information on a wide array of topics and providing communications flows among certain private networks.

World Wide Web - Subsystem of computers providing access to the Internet and offering multimedia and linking capabilities.

Browser - Software supporting the graphics and linking capabilities necessary to navigate the World Wide Web.

Intranet - Private network of internal Websites and other sources of information available to a company's employees.

TRUE AND FALSE QUESTIONS

F 1.   Both bookkeepers and accountants collect, analyze, and measure business performances and translate these measures into information for management decision.

T 2.   Business managers use accounting information to set goals, develop plans, set budgets, and evaluate future prospects.

T 3.   Accounting is actually broken down into two fields-financial and managerial.

F 4. All accountants must be certified by the American Institute of Certified Public Accountants to practice.

T 5. Journal transactions are summarized, usually on a monthly basis, in a final record called the ledger.

T 6. The timing of the annual accounting cycle is called the fiscal year.

F 7. One thing for which we can be sure is that the computer will not process incorrect data.

F 8. Today's automated office still has not solidly accepted the fax machines, voice mail or E-mail.

T 9. Fields, records, and files constitute a database.

T 10. Artificial intelligence can be defined as the construction and programming of computers to imitate human thought processes.

MULTIPLE CHOICE QUESTIONS

1. A comprehensive system for collecting, analyzing, and communicating financial information is called:
   a. computing
   b. accounting
   c. bookkeeping
   d. none of the above

2. The head of the accounting system is the:
   a. treasurer
   b. controller
   c. comptroller
   d. all of above

3. The type of accounting that will focus on the activities of the company as a whole, rather than on individual departments or divisions is called:
   a. cost accounting
   b. financial accounting
   c. audit accounting
   d. managerial accounting

4.　The accounting that serves internal users is called:
　　　　a. cost accounting
　　　　b. financial accounting
　　　　c. audit accounting
　　　　d. managerial accounting

5.　As initial records are received, they are sorted and entered into a:
　　　　a. journal
　　　　b. ledger
　　　　c. file
　　　　d. all of the above

6.　Journal transactions are usually summarized on a monthly basis and then recorded in a:
　　　　a. journal
　　　　b. ledger
　　　　c. file
　　　　d. none of the above

7.　Any economic resource that is expected to benefit a firm or an individual who owns it is called a:
　　　　a. liability
　　　　b. back-charge
　　　　c. asset
　　　　d. debit

8.　In bookkeeping, debit and credit refer to the side on which account information is to be entered. The credit side is on the:
　　　　a. left
　　　　b. middle
　　　　c. right
　　　　d. top

9.　The ease in which current assets can or will be converted into cash within a given year is called its:
　　　　a. liquidity
　　　　b. negotiability
　　　　c. accountability
　　　　d. none of the above

10.　Assets that have long-term use or value like land and equipment is called:
　　　　a. variable assets
　　　　b. fixed assets
　　　　c. intangible assets
　　　　d. all of the above

11. Which of the following are long-term liabilities:
    a. accounts payable
    b. accounts receivable
    c. mortgages
    d. inventory

12. A high turnover ratio indicates:
    a. efficient operations
    b. neglected operations
    c. systemized operations
    d. has no real meaning

13. A centralized, organized collection of related data is called a:
    a. database
    b. word processor
    c. spreadsheet
    d. none of the above

14. Office automation refers to the computer-based devices and applications whose function is to enhance the performance of general office activities. An example of one is the:
    a. E-mail
    b. fax
    c. voice mail
    d. all of the above

15. The manager in need of information to oversee the day-to-day operations of the business is the:
    a. low-level manager
    b. middle manager
    c. top manager
    d. human relations manager

ANSWERS TO TRUE AND FALSE QUESTIONS

1. False
2. True
3. True
4. False
5. True
6. True
7. False
8. False
9. True
10. True

ANSWERS TO MULTIPLE CHOICE QUESTIONS

1. B	6. B	11. C
2. D	7. C	12. A
3. B	8. C	13. A
4. D	9. A	14. D
5. A	10. B	15. A

CHAPTER 13
UNDERSTANDING MARKETING PROCESSES AND CONSUMER BEHAVIOR

CHAPTER OVERVIEW

The American Marketing Association defines marketing as "the process of planning and executing the conception, pricing, promotion, and distribution of ideas, goods, and services." They further state that it should satisfy individual and organization objectives. Marketing is concerned with consumer and industrial goods as well as with services and ideas.

Relationship marketing emphasizes lasting relationships with customers and suppliers. A marketing objective is to sell a satisfied customer who will then return to buy again and again. Marketing is affected by many environments: political (foreign and domestic), social (attitudes and habits of the people) and cultural. Immigration, technological advances and globalization of our world economy will make our world a different world in 30 years.

The marketing mix, often called the "Four P's" of marketing are used to implement a strategy for the marketer. Marketing begins with the **Product** - the goods, services or ideas to satisfy the consumer demand. The product must change as the demand changes. **Pricing** - selecting the most appropriate price at which to sell it. **Promotion** - the techniques for communicating information about the product to the buyer. **Place** - placing the product in the proper outlet.

Since marketers must decide on what market they are going to sell to, marketing segmentation becomes necessary. That is the dividing the market into categories of customer types or segments. An example of market segmentation is to recognize how magazines have segmented their market. There are magazines written specifically to attract golfers, tennis players, fitness enthusiasts, or sailboat owners.

Marketing experts identify marketing segments by those common traits that will affect their purchasing decision. Four of the most important are geographic, demographic, psychographic and product-use variables.

One group watched closely are the teenagers who are spending more than teenagers ever have. This group will grow twice as fast as the overall population. Marketers are monitoring teen trend setters in order to stay on the cutting edge of changing fashion. Understanding consumer behavior is important to marketers. They must understand psychological, personal, social and cultural influences of the buyer. Marketers have constructed various models to help understand the consumer. Buying begins when the consumer recognizes a problem or need and seeks information on how to satisfy that need. The consumer evaluates the information gathered and makes the purchase decision. Consumers make both emotional and rational purchase decisions.

Marketing is concerned with the industrial, resellers, government and institutional markets-they all differ from the consumer market. Today marketing is global and products that are accepted in the U.S. may have to be modified to fit local tastes.

CHAPTER OBJECTIVES

1. Define marketing.

2. Explain how market segmentation is used in target marketing.

3. Identify and explain the steps in consumer buying process.

4. Describe how organizational buying behavior differs from consumer buying behavior.

5. Identify the "Four P's" of marketing.

6. Describe psychographic variables.

OPENING VIGNETTE: STILL PARTYING AFTER ALL THESE YEARS?

College students made Fort Lauderdale their haven for spring break giving the city an image of a mecca for debauchery and beer guzzling. When those student grew up, had families and were looking for a vacation spot for their families, they were turned off on the memory of Fort Lauderdale as they knew it.

The Chamber of Commerce used marketing techniques to change the image. They identified a target market, conducted face-to-face promotional trips, developed new promotional strategies, and created advertising campaigns to put their plans into action. They showed tourists pictures of well-dressed sophisticates enjoying cocktails at a beach front restaurant. They explained their goal by saying " if you are thinking about what was, you need to think about what is." Marketing techniques can and are used for many things other than merchandise, here they were used to change a bad image to a good one.

KEY TERMS

Marketing - The process of planning and executing the conception, pricing, promotion, and distribution of ideas, goods, and services to create exchanges that satisfy individual and organizational objectives.

Consumer goods - Products purchased by consumers for personal use.

Industrial goods - Products purchased by companies to produce other products.

Services - Intangible products, such as time, expertise, or an activity, that can be purchased.

Relationship marketing - Marketing strategy that emphasizes lasting relationships with customers and suppliers.

External environment - Outside factors that influence marketing programs by posing opportunities or threats.

Substitute product - Product that is dissimilar to those of competitors but that can fulfill the same need.

Brand competition - Competitive marketing that appeals to consumer perceptions of similar products.

International competition - Competitive marketing of domestic products against foreign products.

Marketing mix - The combination of product, pricing, promotion, and distribution strategies used to market products.

Product - Food, service, or idea that is marketed to fill consumer needs and wants.

Product differentiation - Creation of a product or product image that differs enough from existing products to attract customers.

Distribution - Part of the marketing mix concerned with getting products from producers to consumers.

Target market - Groups of people that has similar wants and needs and that can be expected to show interest in the same products.

Market segmentation - Process of dividing a market into categories of customer types.

Geographic variables - Geographical units that may be considered in developing a segmentation strategy.

Demographic variables - Characteristics of populations that may be considered in developing a segmentation strategy.

Psychographic variables - Consumer characteristics, such as lifestyles, opinions, interests, and attitudes, that may be considered in developing a segmentation strategy.

Product use variables - Consumer characteristics based on the ways in which a product is used, the brand loyalty it enjoys, and the reasons for which it is purchased.

Consumer behavior - Various facets of the decision process by which customers come to purchase and consume products.

Rational motives - Reasons for purchasing a product that are based on a logical evaluation of product attributes.

Emotional motives - Reasons for purchasing a product that are based on nonobjective factors.

Industrial market - Organizational market consisting of firms that buy goods that are either converted into products or used during production.

Reseller market - Organizational market consisting of intermediaries who buy and resell finished goods.

Institutional market - Organizational market consisting of such nongovernmental buyers of goods and services as hospitals, churches, museums, and charitable organizations.

Derived demand - Demand for industrial products that results from demand for consumer products.

Inelastic demand - Demand for industrial products that is not largely affected by price changes.

TRUE AND FALSE QUESTIONS

1. The marketing mix does not concern itself with developing a product to be sold.

2. Products that are used by companies to produce other products are called industrial goods.

3. Businesses can control internal environments more effectively than external environments.

4. It is expected that Hispanics will make up 24.5 percent of the population of U.S. by 2050.

5. Product differentiation means changing a product's function.

6. Target markets are groups of people with different needs and wants.

7. Psychographic variables describe populations, including such traits as age, income, gender, ethnic background, race and religion.

8. Demographic variables describe life styles, opinions, interest and attitudes.

9. The consumer buying process follows this route: need recognition, information seeking, evaluation and purchase and then postpurchase evaluations.

10. The organizational buyer's decision process follows this route: developing product specifications, evaluating alternatives, purchasing, and making postpurchase evaluations.

MULTIPLE CHOICE QUESTIONS

1. The principles of marketing can be applied to:
   a. consumer goods
   b. industrial goods
   c. services
   d. all of the above

2. Internal environment includes:
   a. employee environment
   b. political environment
   c. economic environment
   d. all of the above

3. Economic conditions:
   a. determine spending patterns by consumers
   b. influence marketer's plans
   c. influence promotional strategies
   d. all of above

4. Which of these promotions is not paid for by the firm:
   a. advertising
   b. personal selling
   c. publicity
   d. public relations

5. Geographic variables deal with peoples:
   a. incomes
   b. ethnic backgrounds
   c. living neighborhoods
   d. gender differences

6. Product-use variables include:
   a. the ways in which consumers use a product
   b. consumer brand loyalty
   c. reasons for purchasing it
   d. all of the above.

7. Psychological influences include:
   a. motivations and attitude
   b. life style
   c. personality
   d. economic status

8. The way of living that distinguishes one large group from another is an example of:
   a. cultural influences
   b. social influences
   c. personal influences
   d. psychological influences

9. The industrial market includes businesses that buy goods falling into the following categories:
   a. goods to be converted into other products
   b. goods that are used up during production
   c. goods sold to farmers
   d. all of the above.

10. Which of the following is incorrect about organizational buyers:
    a. they are trained in buyer-seller relationships
    b. they buy emotionally
    c. they buy rationally
    d. they buy as company specialist in the line of items

11. When an organization places a market into specific categories of customer types, it is called:
    a. market segmentation
    b. geographic segmentation
    c. psychological segmentation
    d. all of above

12. The fastest-growing segment of Americas's population during the next decade will be:
    a. aging baby boomers
    b. new generation baby busters
    c. over 65 age group
    d. new born

13. Personal influences are the cultural ranking of groups according to such criteria as:
    a. backgrounds
    b. occupations
    c. income
    d. life style

14. Relationship marketing means:
    a. having customers return to buy again
    b. taking the customer out for cocktails
    c. offering as little service as possible
    d. all of the above

15. The number of Hispanic-owned businesses in the U.S. surged 76% in five years, proliferating nearly___times as fast as business overall:
    a. six
    b. three
    b. five
    c. two

ANSWERS TO TRUE AND FALSE QUESTIONS

1. False	6. False
2. True	7. False
3. True	8. False
4. True	9. True
5. False	10. True

ANSWERS TO MULTIPLE CHOICE QUESTIONS

1. D	6. D	11. A
2. A	7. A	12. A
3. D	8. A	13. D
4. C	9. D	14. A
5. C	10. B	15. B

CHAPTER 14
DEVELOPING, PRICING, AND PROMOTING PRODUCTS

CHAPTER OVERVIEW

Customers buy a product because they like what the product can do for them, either physically or emotionally. The qualities of the product are its features, what the product does for the consumer is its benefit. In buying a product, consumers are also buying an image and a reputation. Goods and services are broken down into consumer products and industrial products.

Convenience goods like milk, are bought without much comparison shopping. A car is considered shopping goods because most likely one will shop around to compare the product, price and service before buying. Specialty goods are those for which no substitute is acceptable. A group of products that a company makes available for sale is called a product mix. A product line consists of many products within the brand name (i.e.: GE makes refrigerators and many more appliances). No firm can count on a single successful product to carry it forever.

When a company contemplates developing a new product it must consider the products mortality rate, and how long it takes to move the product from the laboratory to the marketplace. All products have a life cycle: the introductory period when there is little competition, the growth period follows when it attracts enough customers and profits are high. In its maturity stage competition is fierce, and sales and profits are more difficult to achieve. The products decline stage is in its last stage before it is no longer a viable product.

Products are given brand names to make it easier for customers to choose the product. There are national brands, like Coca Cola, licensed brands, like the many Mickey Mouse products on sale, and the private brands just sold by individual stores. The packaging of a brand helps sell the product.

Pricing to maximize profits, pricing to get a fair share of the market, and pricing to meet the competition, are pricing objectives. These are the goals the seller hopes to attain in selling the product. When introducing a new product, skimming strategy may be used where prices are set high in order to earn a large profit on each item sold. The penetration strategy seeks to sell as many items as possible at lower prices to generate consumer interest. Pricing tactics include price lining, psychological pricing and discounting of prices.

Promotion has four goals to achieve. It is designed to sell a product, communicate information, position a product and control the sales volume. A pull strategy attempts to motivate the consumer to demand the product in the retail store, while the push strategy goal is to have the wholesaler and retailer get the consumer to buy the product.

The promotional mix consists of advertising, personal selling, sales promotion, publicity and public relations. The best combination of these tools is called the promotional mix.

CHAPTER OBJECTIVES

1. Differentiate between consumer and industrial products.

2. Explain the different pricing objectives.

3. Describe the pricing strategies and tactics used to sell a product.

4. Identify the objectives of promotion and explain how one can utilize the promotional mix.

5. Describe the major advertising media available to a company.

6. Differentiate and give examples of advertising and publicity.

7. Explain and give examples of the life cycle of a product.

8. Explain the differences between a price mix and a price line.

OPENING VIGNETTE: CHARTING THE AIR JORDAN ROUTE

With a carefully crafted marketing strategy, Nike introduces a new Air Jordan sneaker. The Chicago Bulls' Michael Jordan uses the new sneakers during games and acts as its spokesman. It restricts the supply of these new sneakers, thus causing a shortage, and at the same time increases the demand and generates enough excitement among the target market-- teenagers--to convince them to pay $115 a pair.

Nike produces 12 different versions of Air Jordans. The way Nike markets Air Jordan sneakers provides insight into the unique requirements of developing, pricing and promoting a product.

KEY TERMS

Convenience good/service - Relatively inexpensive product purchased and consumed rapidly and regularly.

Shopping good/service - Moderately expensive, infrequently purchased product.

Specialty good/service - Expensive, rarely purchased product.

Expense item - Relatively inexpensive industrial product purchased and consumed rapidly and regularly.

Capital item - Expensive, durable, infrequently purchased industrial product, such as a building and machinery.

Product mix - group of products that a firm makes available for sale.

Product line - Group of similar products intended for a similar group of buyers that will use them in similar ways.

Product life cycle (PLC) - Series of stages in a product's profit-producing life.

Branding - Process of using symbols to communicate the qualities of a product made by a particular producer.

National brand - Brand-name product produced by, widely distributed by, and carrying the name of the manufacturer.

Licensed brand - Brand-name product for whose name the seller has purchased the right from an organization or individual.

Private brand (or Private label) - Brand-name product that a wholesaler or retailer has commissioned from a manufacturer.

Packaging - Physical container in which a product is sold, advertised, and/or protected.

Pricing - Process of determining what a company will receive in exchange for its products.

Pricing objectives - Goals that producers hope to attain in pricing products for sale.

Market share - Sales of an individual company as a percentage of total sales in a particular market.

Mark-up - Amount added to a product's cost in order to sell it at a profit.

Variable cost - Cost that changes with the quantity of a product produced or sold.

Fixed cost - Cost unaffected by the quantity of a product produced or sold.

Break-even analysis - Assessment of the quantity of a product that must be sold before the seller makes a profit.

Break-even point - Quantity of a product that must be sold before the seller covers variable and fixed costs and makes a profit.

Price leader - Dominant firm that establishes product prices that other companies follow.

Price skimming - Setting the initial price high enough to cover new product costs and generate a profit.

Penetration pricing - Setting the initial price low in order to establish a new product in the market.

Price lining - Setting a limited number of prices for certain categories of products.

Psychological pricing - Pricing tactic that takes advantage of the fact that consumers don not always respond rationally to stated prices.

Odd-even pricing - Psychological pricing tactic based on the premise that customers prefer prices not stated in even dollar amounts.

Discount - Price reduction offered as an incentive to purchase.

Promotion - Aspect of the marketing mix concerned with the most effective techniques for selling a product.

Positioning - Process of establishing an identifiable product image in the minds of consumers.

Pull strategy - Promotional strategy designed to appeal directly to customers, who will demand a product from retailers.

Push strategy - Promotional strategy designed to encourage wholesalers and/or retailers to market products to consumers.

Promotional mix - Combination of tools used to promote a product.

Advertising - Promotional tool consisting of paid, nonpersonal communication used by an identified sponsor to inform an audience about a product.

Advertising media - Variety of communication services for carrying a seller's message to potential customers.

Media mix - Combination of advertising media chosen to carry messages about a product.

Direct mail - Advertising medium in which messages are mailed directly to consumers.

Personal selling - Promotional tool in which a salesperson communicates one to one with potential customers.

Sales promotion - Short-term promotional activity designed to stimulate consumer buying or cooperation from distributors and sales agents.

TRUE AND FALSE QUESTIONS

1.   Features are the qualities, tangible and intangible, that a company "builds into" its product.

2.   Shopping goods customers will not accept substitutes for what they want.

3.   Convenience goods are consumed rapidly and regularly and customers spend little time selecting them.

4.   Capital items are permanent, long lasting and expensive.

5.   An example of a product line is the fact that General Electric makes washing machines, refrigerators and other major appliances under its own name.

6.   The growth stage in a products life cycle is when sales begin to slow down.

7.   An example of a licensed brand is the Hard Rock Cafe permitting sweat shirt manufacturers to use their name on its shirts.

8.   The difference between what a product costs and what it sells for is called a mark-up and it is usually stated as a percentage of cost.

9.   Price skimming seeks to generate consumer interest and stimulate trial purchase of new products.

10.   Selling gasoline for $1.45.9 is an example of psychological pricing.

MULTIPLE CHOICE QUESTIONS

1. In buying a product consumers are also buying:
   a. an image
   b. a reputation
   c. a benefit
   d. all of above

2. A product that is consumed rapidly and regularly such as those offered by a fast food restaurant is called:
   a. a convenience good
   b. a shopping good
   c. a specialty good
   d. none of the above

3. An example of a capital item would be:
   a. factory building
   b. advertising budget
   c. wages and benefits
   d all of the above

4. An example of a product line is:
   a. Coca Cola
   b. Ford Motor Cars
   c. Tootsie rolls
   d. Harley-Davidson Motorcycles

5. On the product life cycle the Cellular telephone is on which step:
   a. Introduction
   b. Growth
   c. Maturity
   d. Decline

6. Colorado Jeans is an example of:
   a. National brand
   b. licensed brand
   c. private brand
   d. none of the above

7. The movie Forrest Gump invented a company called Bubba Gump Seafood. Today we see shrimp cans, baseball caps and bubble gum with that name on it. This is an example of a:
    a. national brand
    b. licensed brand
    c. private brand
    d. none of the above

8. A product must have a package to hold the ingredients but it also plays a part in:
    a. store advertisement
    b. making the product attractive
    c. displaying the brand name
    d. all of the above

9. Costs that change with the number of goods or services produced or sold are called:
    a. profit makers
    b. variable
    c. fixed
    d. none of the above

10. An example of pricing above prevailing market prices for similar products are:
    a. Bloomingdales
    b. Godiva chocolates
    c. Rolls-Royce
    d. all of the above

11. A company that establishes a product price that others follow is called a:
    a. price buster
    b. price leader
    c. price fixer
    d. price skimmer

12. The text states that consumers have a feeling about negotiating a price for a product, they:
    a. want to negotiate prices
    b. want a no haggle dealing
    c. don't know what they want
    d. take what ever is offered to them

13. The ultimate objective of any promotion is to increase sales. In addition, however it also uses promotion to:
    a. communicate information
    b. position a product
    c. control sales volume
    d. all of the above

14. The part of promotion that is "free" is :
    a. advertising
    b. personal selling
    c. sales promotion
    d. publicity

15. The most widely used medium in advertising, accounting for about 25 percent of all expenditures is:
    a. TV
    b. radio
    c. newspapers
    d. magazines

ANSWERS TO TRUE AND FALSE QUESTIONS

1. True	6. False
2. False	7. True
3. True	8. False
4. True	9. False
5. True	10. True

ANSWERS TO MULTIPLE CHOICE QUESTIONS

1. D	6. C	11. B
2. A	7. B	12. A
3. A	8. D	13. D
4. B	9. B	14. D
5. B	10. D	15. C

CHAPTER 15
DISTRIBUTING PRODUCTS

CHAPTER OVERVIEW

Manufacturers produce merchandise in great quantities and must sell the output in large quantities. Retailers sell these products one item at a time to consumers, and thus can only buy a small quantity of the merchandise produced. How can this conflict be reconciled when retailers must get the merchandise on-time, at the right quantity and at the right price? The answer is intermediaries using various distribution strategies. Once called middlemen, intermediaries are the individuals and firms who help to distribute the producer's goods.

A distribution channel is the path that a product follows from producer to end user. Selecting the appropriate distribution network is a vital consideration. Different degrees of market exposure are available through strategies of intensive, exclusive, and selective distribution.

Channel conflict occurs when members of the channel disagree over the roles they should play or the rewards they should receive. Usually one channel member, the most powerful (best customer) determines the roles and rewards for other members.

Wholesaling, in addition to storing and providing an assortment of products adds value for customers by offering delivery, credit, and product information. There are merchant wholesalers, limited function merchant wholesalers, agents and brokers.

There are over 2.5 million retail establishments in the United States. Over 50 percent of them are small and account for less than 10 percent of all retail sales. Retail types are: department store, supermarkets, hypermarkets, and specialty stores. Retailers who specialize in bargain prices are: discount houses, off-price stores, catalog showrooms, factory outlets and warehouse clubs.

Non-store retailing continues to grow with vending machines, direct-response retailers, mail marketing, video marketing, telemarketing, electronic shopping and direct selling. On-line retailing, via the Internet, is in its infancy, the infant is growing by leaps and bounds.

Physical distribution refers to the activities needed to move products efficiently from manufacturers to consumers, and include such activities as warehousing and transporting operations. Many different types of warehousing are available each offering different services. The mode of transportation chosen depends on the cost or speed of delivery required. Those available are: truck, railroads, planes, water carriers or pipelines. Distribution costs have fallen in recent years and delivery times have been reduced due to new innovations.

CHAPTER OBJECTIVES

1. Explain the functions of the different channels of distribution.

2. Describe the duties of the three distribution strategies.

3. Explain how wholesaling adds value to customers.

4. Identify the different types of wholesalers and explain how their duties differ.

5. Differentiate between the different types of retailers.

6. Compare the five basic forms of transportation.

7. Describe the major activities in physical distribution.

OPENING VIGNETTE:
THE BATTLE PLAN FOR ATTACKING INVENTORY AT THE BIG STORE

During the Persian Gulf War, three-star Army General William G. Pagonis managed the largest military logistical operation in history. He supplied the needed resources to the U.S. troops while fighting firestorms, extreme weather conditions, and cultural confusion.

The remarkable logistical achievements during the Persian Gulf War convinced the Sears, Roebuck & Company president that General Pagonis could do the same for Sears. Once called "the stepchild of the retail industry," logistics has become a major concern for retailers. Logistics--or distribution management--involves goods from supplier to warehouse to store to customer.

Pagonis was hired by Sears and attacked the status-quo with military zeal. He reduced the number of channels used by store managers to order products from 12 to 4 and increased the average load carried by delivery trucks leaving Sears distribution centers from 60 to 90 percent.

Customers can now choose among morning, afternoon, and evening deliveries. It now takes seven days instead of 14 days to ship apparel from supplier to stores. Fast delivery lowers the need to stock the inventory in larger quantities. This vignette exemplifies the fact that retailers who use the up-to-date logistical techniques can save money, increase customer satisfaction and lower inventory costs. It proves that any organization can gain from using logistics wisely.

KEY TERMS

Distribution mix - The combination of distribution channels by which a firm gets its products to end users.

Intermediary - Individual or firm that helps to distribute a product

Wholesaler - Intermediary that sells products to other businesses for resale to final consumers.

Retailer - Intermediary that sells products directly to consumers.

Distribution channel - Network of interdependent companies through which a product passes from producer to end user.

Direct channel - Distribution channel in which a product travels from producer to consumer without intermediaries.

Sales agent/broker - Independent intermediary that usually represents many manufacturers a and sells to wholesalers, retailers, or both.

Industrial distribution - Network of channel members involved in the flow of manufactured goods to industrial customers.

Sales office - Office maintained by a manufacturer as a contact point with its customers.

Merchant wholesaler - Independent wholesaler that takes legal possession of goods produced by a variety of manufacturers and then resells them to other businesses.

Full-service merchant wholesaler - Merchant wholesaler that provides credit, marketing, and merchandising services in addition to traditional buying and selling services.

Limited-function merchant wholesaler - Merchant wholesaler that provides a limited range of services.

Drop shipper - Limited-function merchant wholesaler that receives customer orders, negotiates with producers, takes title to goods, and arranges for shipment to customers.

Rack jobber - Limited-function merchant wholesaler that sets up and maintains display racks in retail stores.

Department store - Large product-line retailer characterized by organization into specialized departments.

Supermarket - Large product-line retailer offering a variety of food and food-related items in specialized departments.

Hypermarket - Very large product-line retailer carrying a wide variety of unrelated products.

Scrambled merchandising - Retail practice of carrying any product expected to sell well regardless of a store's original product offering.

Specialty store - Small retail store carrying one product line or category of related products.

Bargain retailer- Retailer carrying a wide range of products at bargain prices.

Discount house - Bargain retailer that generates large sales volume by offering goods at substantial price reductions.

Off-price stores - Bargain retailer that buys excess inventories from high-quality manufacturers and sells them at discounted prices.

Catalog showroom - Bargain retailer in which customers place orders for catalog items to be picked up at on-premise warehouses.

Factory outlet - Bargain retailer owned by the manufacturer whose products it sells.

Warehouse club (or **Wholesale club**) - Bargain retailer offering large discounts on brand-name merchandise to customers who have paid annual membership fees.

Direct response retailing - Nonstore retailing by direct interaction with customers to inform them of products and receive sales orders.

Mail order (or **Catalog marketing**) - Nonstore retailing in which customers place orders for catalog merchandise received through the mail.

Video marketing - Nonstore retailing to consumers via standard and cable television.

Telemarketing - Nonstore retailing in which the telephone is used to sell directly to consumers.

Electronic shopping - Nonstore retailing in which information about the seller's products and services is connected into customers' computers allowing consumers to receive the information and purchase the products in the home.

Direct selling - Form of nonstore retailing typified by door-to-door sales.

Physical distribution - Movement of a product from manufacturer to consumer.

Warehousing - Physical distribution operation concerned with the storage of goods.

Private warehouse - Warehouse owned by and providing storage for a single company.

Public warehouse - Independently owned and operated warehouse that stores goods for many firms.

Storage warehouse - Warehouse providing storage for extended periods of time.

Distribution center - Warehouse providing shirt-term storage of goods for which demand is both constant and high.

Inventory control - Warehouse operation that tracks inventory on hand and ensures that an adequate supply is in stock at all times.

Materials handling - Warehouse operation involving the transportation, arrangement, and orderly retrieval of goods in inventory.

Intermodal transportation - Combined use of several different modes of transportation.

Containerization - Transportation method in which goods are sealed in containers at shipping sources and opened when they reach final destinations.

Common carrier - Transporting company, such as a truck line or railroad, that transports goods for any shipper.

Freight forwarder - Transporting company that leases bulk space from other carriers to be resold to firms making smaller shipments.

Contract carrier - Independent transporting company that usually owns the vehicles in which it transports products.

Private carrier - Manufacturer or retailer that maintains its own transportation system.

Hub - Central distribution outlet that controls all or most of a firm's distribution activities.

TRUE AND FALSE QUESTIONS

1.   Once called middlemen, intermediaries are the individuals and firms who help to distribute a producer's goods.

2.   Retailers and wholesalers are not considered intermediaries.

3.   In a direct channel, the produce travels from the producer to the consumer without intermediaries.

4. Wholesalers have entered the distribution network to take over more and more of the storage services.

5. The more members in the channel--the more intermediaries--the higher the final price.

6. If we eliminated intermediaries, we would eliminate the cost entailed by what they do.

7. Intensive distribution entails distributing a product through as many channels and channel members as possible.

8. Merchant wholesalers purchase and own the goods they resell.

9. The value of agents and brokers lies primarily in their knowledge of markets and their merchandising expertise.

10. Most retailers are small, and make up over 50 percent of all retail establishments and make 60 percent of U.S. retail sales.

MULTIPLE CHOICE QUESTIONS

1. Retailers that feature broad product lines include:
    a. specialty stores
    b. department stores
    c. supermarkets
    d. all of the above

2. Stores that carry one line of related merchandise are called:
    a. hypermarkets
    b. specialty stores
    c. category killers
    d. warehouse stores

3. The type of retailer who buys the excess inventories of well-recognized high-quality manufacturers and sells them at prices up to 60 percent lower than regular department stores are called:
    a. discount stores
    b. off-price stores
    c. catalog stores
    d. factory outlets

4. The retail store that charges membership fees to its customers is called a:
    a. discount store
    b. off-price store
    c. warehouse club
    d. convenience store

5. The following non-store retailer does business mainly through the mails:
    a. direct response retailer
    b. telemarketing retailer
    c. direct mail retailer
    d. electronic retailer

6. The use of the computer-information system that allows sellers to connect into consumers' computers with information about products is called:
    a. telemarketing
    b. electronic shopping
    c. video shopping
    d. catalog shopping

7. Possibly the oldest form of retailing is:
    a. direct selling
    b. factory outlet selling
    c. mail selling
    d. none of the above

8. Activities such as warehousing and transporting operations are included in the duties of:
    a. physical distribution
    b. sales promotion
    c. personal selling
    d. direct selling

9. Warehouses that are owned and used by one company are called:
    a. public warehouses
    b. distribution centers
    c. private warehouses
    d. all of the above

10. The highest cost faced by many manufacturers is the cost of:
    a. personal selling
    b. advertising
    c. packaging
    d. physically moving a product

11. The least expensive mode of transporting goods is the:
   a. railroad
   b. truck
   c. waterway
   d. pipeline

12. If it transports products for any firm for a contracted price and time period it is called a:
   a. common carrier
   b. freight forwarder
   c. contract carrier
   d. none of the above

13. If it leases bulk space from other carriers, such as railroads or airlines it is called a:
   a. common carrier
   b. freight forwarder
   c. contract carrier
   d. none of the above.

14. Supply-side hubs make the most sense when large shipments of supplies flow regularly to a single industrial user, such as:
   a. manufacturer
   b. retailer
   c. wholesaler
   d. warehouse

15. The distributing of a product through as many channels and channel members as possible is called:
   a. exclusive distribution
   b. intensive distribution
   c. neutral distribution
   d. selective distribution

ANSWERS TO TRUE AND FALSE QUESTIONS

1. True	6. False
2. False	7. True
3. True	8. True
4. True	9. True
5. True	10. False

ANSWERS TO MULTIPLE CHOICE QUESTIONS

1. D	6. B	11. D
2. B	7. A	12. C
3. B	8. A	13. B
4. C	9. C	14. A
5. C	10. D	15. A

CHAPTER 16
UNDERSTANDING MONEY AND BANKING

CHAPTER OVERVIEW

The characteristics of money the world over are the same. Whether it is a French franc, or a Japanese yen, it must have portability, be divisible, durable and stable. In broad terms money serves three functions: as a medium of exchange, a store of value and a unit of account. We should be able to exchange a dollar bill for a dollars worth of material, know that the dollar will buy a similar value in the near future and be able to have a record of our financial worth.

In the U.S. the supply of money is measured by the "M-1", that is spendable money in forms of currency, demand deposits and other checkable deposits. Checking account owners can write a check on their money in the bank at any time and "demand" the money. Two examples of a time deposit which cannot be withdrawn by check are the "CD" and saving certificates. They have a specific time when the funds are not available to the depositor and usually pay a higher interest rate than regular savings accounts..

Investment companies have money market mutual funds where assets are pooled from many investors. Interest payment is usually higher on these accounts. Credit cards the "plastic money" is also very popular although not technically money.

The main function of financial institutions is to ease the flow of money from areas of surplus to areas of deficits. There are over 100,000 commercial banks carrying a charter from the federal or state government. Every bank receives a major portion of its income from interest paid on loans by borrowers. There are savings and loan associations, mutual savings banks, credit unions and nondeposit institutions. Examples of nondeposit institutions are pension funds, insurance companies, finance companies and securities dealers.

Due to bank failures during the depression, the U.S. government set up the Federal Deposit Insurance Corporation that insures up to $100,000 of depositors funds. The Federal Reserve System regulates many aspects of our banking structure. All nationally chartered commercial banks are members of the Federal Reserve System. The Fed as it is called, controls the money supply, regulates the number of banking activities, and issues charters to banks. By controlling the money supply the Fed can loosen up the supply of money when needed or tighten it when inflation appears likely.

Banking deregulation rules were passed in 1980 to make banking more competitive. It permitted interstate banking for the fist time. Banks are investing in electronic technologies and are issuing credit cards, debit cards and point-of-sale terminals. Smart cards are becoming affordable, E-cash can be moved outside the established networks of banks, checks and paper currency. It is said that by the year 2005 as much as 20% of all household expenditures will take place on the Internet.

The International Bank Structure is made up of the World Bank and the International Monetary Fund which helps to finance international trade. Their objectives are to promote stability of exchange rates, offer short-term loans to countries and to encourage members to cooperate on international monetary issues.

CHAPTER OBJECTIVES

1. Define the term money and identify the different forms it takes.

2. Explain the four criteria of money.

3. Describe the three functions of money and give examples of each.

4. Describe what the U.S. government has done recently to stop the counterfeiting of U.S. currency.

5. Differentiate between time and demand deposits.

6. Explain the differences between Savings and Loan Associations, Mutual Saving Banks, Credit Unions and Non-deposit institutions.

7. Describe how the Federal Reserve Bank controls the money supply of banks.

OPENING VIGNETTE: ACCOUNTING FOR SOUTH AFRICA'S "UNBANKED"

Impoverished, illiterate blacks who were virtually ignored as potential customers in the old South Africa are being served for the first time by financial institutions that see opportunity in serving this vast, untapped market.

Collectively, the domestic workers, peddlers, and day laborers who make up South Africa's informal economy, control millions of dollars in cash. These potential customers need basic services that provide an easy way to deposit and withdraw money. Having access to banking facilities offers these poor blacks peace of mind.

As poor blacks open bank accounts for the first time, they are seen as individuals with money of their own and it brings them into the institutional fabric of the society. The banks have taken these deposits and invested the funds in home loans for black customers. The bank had the problem of dealing with a citizenship made up of 55 percent illiterate unsophisticated banking customers who were taught to use the ATM card by local bank clerks. Ironically, high technology gives the bank the ability to market to poorly educated consumers. They have developed machines that can be worked without being able to read and write. Banking has come into the technological age earning profits for the bank and offering needed services to the people.

KEY TERMS

Money - Any object that is portable, divisible, durable, and stable and that serves as a medium of exchange, a store of value, and a unit of account.

M-1 - Measure of the money supply that includes only the most liquid (spendable) forms of money.

Currency - Government-issued paper money and metal coins.

Check - Demand deposit order instructing a bank to pay a given sum to a specified payee.

Demand deposits - Bank account funds that may be withdrawn at any time.

M-2 - Measure of the money supply that includes all the components of M-1 plus forms of money that can easily be converted into spendable form.

Time deposits - Bank funds that cannot be withdrawn without notice or transferred by check.

Money market mutual fund - Fund of short-term, low-risk financial securities purchased with the assets of investors-owned pooled by a nonbank institution.

Commercial bank - Federal- or state-chartered financial institution accepting deposits that it uses to make loans and earn profits.

State bank - Commercial bank chartered by an individual state.

National bank - Commercial bank chartered by the federal government.

Prime rate - Interest rate available to a bank's most creditworthy customers.

Savings and loan association (S&L) - Financial institution accepting deposits and making loans primarily for home mortgages.

Mutual savings bank - Financial institution whose depositors are owners sharing in its profits.

Credit union - Financial institution that accepts deposits from, and makes loans to, only its members, usually employees of a particular organization.

Pension fund - Nondeposit pool of funds managed to provide retirement income for its members.

Insurance company - Nondeposit institution that invests funds collected as premiums charged for insurance coverage.

Finance company - Nondeposit institution that specializes in making loans to businesses and consumers.

Securities investment dealer (broker) - Nondeposit institution that buys and sells stocks and bonds both for investors and for its own accounts.

Individual retirement account (IRA) - Tax-deferred pension fund with which wage earners supplement other retirement funds.

Keogh plan - Tax-deferred pension plan for the self-employed.

Trust services - Bank management of an individual's investments, payments, or estate.

Letter of credit - Bank promise, issues for a buyer, to pay a designated firm a certain amount of money if specified conditions are met.

Banker's acceptance - Bank promise, issued for a buyer, to pay a designated firm a specified amount at a future date.

Automated teller machine (ATM) - Electronic machine that allows customers to conduct account-related activities 24 hours a day, seven days a week.

Electronic funds transfer (EFT) - Communication of fund transfer information over wire, cable, or microwave.

Federal Deposit Insurance Company (FDIC) - Federal agency that guarantees the safety of bank deposits up to $100,000.

Federal Reserve System (the Fed) - The central bank of the United States, which acts as the governments bank, services member commercial banks, and controls the nation's money supply.

Float - Amount of checks written but not yet cleared through the Federal Reserve.

Monetary policy - Policies by which the Federal Reserve manages the nation's money supply and interest rates.

Reserve requirement - Percentage of deposits a bank must hold in cash or on deposit with the Federal Reserve.

Discount rate - Interest rate at which member banks can borrow money from the Federal Reserve.

Open-market operations - The Federal Reserve's sales and purchases of U.S. government securities in the open market.

Selective credit controls - Federal Reserve authority to set margin requirements for consumer stock purchases and credit rules for other consumer purchases.

Debit card - Plastic card that allows an individual to transfer money between bank accounts.

Point-of-sale (POS) terminal - Electronic device that allows customers to pay for retail purchases with debit cards.

Smart card - Credit card-sized computer that can be programmed with "electronic money".

E-cash - Money that moves among consumers and businesses via digital electronic transmissions.

TRUE AND FALSE QUESTIONS

1. The four criteria of money is portable, divisible, durable and stable.

2. Money makes it possible to barter in the open market.

3. "M-1" counts the money supply that includes only the most liquid forms of money.

4. Bank funds that cannot be withdrawn without notice or transferred by check are called demand deposits.

5. "M-2" includes everything in M-1 plus items which cannot be spent directly but which are easily converted to spendable forms.

6. Money market mutual funds are operated by investment companies that bring together pools of assets from many investors.

7. The Keogh plan is a tax-deferred pension fund with which wage earners supplement other retirement funds.

8. Banks are allowed to loan out all of the money they take in for deposits.

9. The Federal Deposit Insurance Corporation guarantees that the stocks and bonds you invest in will not lose value.

10. All nationally chartered commercial banks are members of the Federal Reserve System as are some state-chartered banks.

MULTIPLE CHOICE QUESTIONS

1. Any object can serve as money if it is:
   a. portable
   b. divisible
   c. durable
   d. all of the above

2. Money should serve the following function:
   a. medium of exchange
   b. store of value
   c. unit of account
   d. all of the above

3. When the money supply is high, the value of money:
   a. drops
   b. raises
   c. remains constant
   d. none of the above

4. The items accepted as currency in the U.S. are:
   a. traveler's checks
   b. credit cards
   c. debit cards
   d. personal checks

5. A check is an example of a:
   a. time deposit
   b. demand deposit
   c. money market fund
   d. savings deposit

6. A bank that accepts deposits which they use to make loans and to earn profits is an example of a:
   a. mutual savings bank
   b. savings and loan association
   c. credit union
   d. commercial bank

7. A bank that accepts deposits only from members who meet specific qualifications, usually working for a particular employer is called a:
   a. mutual savings bank
   b. savings and loan association
   c. credit union
   d. commercial bank

8. A bank that accepts deposits and makes loans primarily for home mortgages is called a:
   a. mutual savings bank
   b. savings and loan association
   c. credit union
   d. commercial bank

9. A bank where all depositors are considered owners of the bank is called a:
   a. mutual savings bank
   b. savings and loan association
   c. credit union
   d. commercial bank

10. An organization that buys and sells stocks and bonds on the New York and other stock exchanges for clients investors is called a:
    a. insurance company
    b. finance company
    c. securities dealer
    d. all of the above

11. A service of the Federal Reserve Bank is to:
    a. cover accounts by the FDIC
    b. clear checks
    c. produce the nation's paper currency
    d. all of the above

12. To control the money supply, the Fed uses the following tool or tools:
        a. discount-rate controls
        b. open-market operations
        c. selective credit controls
        d. all of the above

13. The Fed loans money to banks and the interest rate of these loans is known as:
        a. charge rates
        b. reserve rates
        c. discount rates
        d. all of the above

14. The act that allowed banks to enter into interstate banking is called:
        a. Pepper-McFadden Act
        b. Depository Institutions Deregulation Control Act
        c. Interstate Banking Efficiency Act
        d. Citibank Expansion Act

15. Debit cards allow the transfer of money between:
        a. bank and store
        b. customer and bank
        c. checking account and savings account
        d. none of the above

ANSWERS TO TRUE AND FALSE QUESTIONS

1. True	6. True
2. False	7. False
3. True	8. False
4. False	9. False
5. True	10. True

ANSWERS TO MULTIPLE CHOICE QUESTIONS

1. D	6. D	11. D
2. D	7. C	12. D
3. A	8. B	13. C
4. A	9. A	14. C
5. B	10. C	15. A

CHAPTER 17
UNDERSTANDING SECURITIES AND INVESTMENTS

CHAPTER OVERVIEW

Stocks and bonds are known as securities because they represent secured, or asset-based claims on the part of investors. Bonds represent strictly financial claims for money owed to holders by a company, common stocks represent ownership of a corporation. The market where stocks and bonds are sold is called securities market. When a corporation first desires to sell securities it must get the permission of the Security and Exchange Commission and then sell an initial public offering. IPO's give corporations a cash boost for growth.

Stock values are expressed in three different ways, as par, market and book value. When one sells stock for a higher price than when purchased, it is called a capital gain. Common stocks are among the riskiest of all securities but offer high growth potential. Blue chip stocks are from well-established firms. Preferred stock has a par value set on it and may be callable, which calls for shareholders to surrender the stock upon request. The call price is an agreed price between the firm and its stockholders.

Stocks and bonds are purchased through a stock exchange. Only members (or their representatives) of the stock exchange are allowed to trade on the exchange. Brokers receive and execute buy and sell orders from nonexchange members. The two major stock exchanges in the U.S. are the New York and American Stock Exchange. There are also regional stock exchanges. Foreign stock exchanges are found in London, Tokyo and other cities. The over-the-counter market has no trading floor and is located in different locations linked by electronic communications.

The U.S. bond market is supplied by three major sources: the U.S. government, municipalities and corporations. Unsecured corporation bonds are called debentures. The three types of bonds are: callable, serial, and convertible. Other investment types are mutual funds and commodities. Some investors purchase securities on margin, paying only a percentage of the cost, giving them an opportunity to buy more since a large proportion of the purchase is on credit. Newspapers list the daily transactions of the stock exchange so that investors can keep track of their investments. The Dow and Standard and Poor's reports stock price movements. An individual may purchase stock from one of the many stock brokers found in the yellow pages of the telephone book.

CHAPTER OBJECTIVES

1. Differentiate between the various types of bonds in terms of their safety, issuers and retirement.

2. Explain the differences between the primary and secondary securities market.

3. Describe the differences between a mutual fund and buying a stock on ones own.

4. Explain the meaning of stock values as expressed as par, market and book value.

5. Differentiate between the three types of bonds: U.S. government, municipalities and corporations.

6. Describe the four types of attitudes toward investment risks.

7. Explain the meanings of the various columns in the newspapers stock quotations.

OPENING VIGNETTE:
WHY WALL STREET DOESN'T SCARE THE DICKENS OUT OF EVERYONE

To appreciate the extent to which the average American has entered into the stock market, just compare the 6 million people who owned stocks in the 1950's to the 50 million today. Individuals are investing their discretionary money and retirement pensions into equities. More "average" Americans are taking the initiative to plan their own future and more will also be hurt if there is a market crash.

Investment clubs, individual investors salting away funds in equities rather than banks and monthly "Christmas Club" investors are preparing for tomorrow by buying equities. While prices continue to climb, all is well, but what happens when the market does fall? Almost half of the investors said they would remain steady, ten percent said it would give them an opportunity to buy more stock at a reduced price, and 20 percent said they would sell.

With stocks representing an increasingly important share of a family's finances, experts predict that hordes of investors would panic at a crash. When investing in stocks, one always thinks of the profits, but seldom on how to handle a "correction." It is important not to join the hordes who panic.

KEY TERMS

Securities - Stocks and bonds representing secured, or asset-based, claims by investors against issuers.

Primary securities market - Market in which new stocks and bonds are bought and sold.

Investment bank - Financial institution engaged in issuing and reselling new securities.

Secondary securities market - Market in which stocks and bonds are traded.

Par value - Face value of a share of stock, set by the issuing company's board of directors.

Market value - Current price of a share of stock in the stock market.

Capital gain - Profit earned by selling a share of stock for more than it cost.

Book value - Value of a common stock expressed as total shareholders' equity dividend by the number of shares of stock.

Blue chip stock - Common stock issued by a well-established company with a sound financial history and a stable pattern of dividend payouts.

Cumulative preferred stock - Preferred stock on which dividends not paid in the past must be paid to stockholders before dividends can be paid to common stockholders.

Stock exchange - Organization of individuals formed to provide an institutional setting in which stock can be traded.

Broker - Individual or organization who receives an executes buy and sell orders on behalf of other people in return for commissions.

Over-the-counter (OTC) market - Organization of securities dealers formed to trade stock outside the formal institutional setting of the organized stock exchanges.

National Association of Securities Dealers Automated Quotation (NASDAQ) system - Organization of over-the-counter dealers who own, buy, and sell their own securities over a network of electronic communications.

Bond - Security through which an issuer promises to pay the buyer a certain amount of money by a specified future date.

Government bond - Bond issued by the federal government.

Municipal bond - Bond issued by a state or local government.

Corporate bond - Bond issued by a company as a source of long-term funding.

Registered bond - Bond bearing the name of the holder and registered with the issuing company.

Bearer (or Coupon) bond - Bond requiring the holder to clip and submit a coupon in order to receive an interest payment.

Secured bond - Bond backed by pledges of assets to the bondholders.

Debenture - Unsecured bond for which no specific property is pledged as security.

Mutual fund - Company that pools investments from individuals and organizations to purchase a portfolio of stocks, bonds, and short-term securities.

No-load fund - Mutual fund in which investors are charged sales commissions when they buy in or sell out.

Futures contract - Agreement to purchase specified amounts of a commodity at a given price on a set future date.

Commodities market - Market in which futures contracts are traded.

Margin - Percentage of the total sales price that a buyer must put up to place an order for stock or futures contracts.

Price-earnings ratio - Current price of a stock divided by the firm's current annual earnings per share.

Bid price - Price that an OTC broker pays for a share of stock.

Asked price - Price that an OTC broker charges for a share of stock.

Market index - Summary of price trends in a specific industry and/or the stock market as a whole.

Bull market - Period of rising stock prices.

Bear market - Period of falling stock prices.

Dow Jones Industrial Average - Market index based on the prices of 30 of the largest industrial firms listed on the NYSE.

Standard & Poor's Composite Index - Market index based on the performance of 400 industrial firms, 40 utilities, 40 financial institutions, and 20 transportation companies.

Market order - Order to buy or sell a security at the market price prevailing at the time the order is placed.

Limit order - Order authorizing the purchase of a stock only if its price is equal to or less than a specified amount.

Stop order - Order authorizing the sale of a stock if its price falls to or below a specified level.

Round lot - Purchase or sale of stock in units of 100 shares.

Odd lot - Purchase or sale of stock in fractions of round lots.

Short sale - Stock sale in which an investor borrows securities from a broker to be sold and then replaced at a specified future date.

Program trading - Large purchase or sale of a group of stocks, often triggered by computerized trading programs that can be launched without human supervision or control.

Securities and Exchange Commission (SEC) - Federal agency that administers U.S. securities laws to protect the investing public and maintain smoothly functioning markets.

Prospectus - Registration statement filed with the SEC before the issuance of a new security.

Insider trading - Illegal practice of using special knowledge about a firm for profit or gain.

Blue sky laws - Laws requiring securities dealers to be licensed and registered with the states in which they do business.

TRUE AND FALSE QUESTIONS

1.   Stocks and bonds represent secured, or asset-based, claims by investors against issuers.

2.   Merril Lynch and Morgan Stanley provide underwriting functions and thus bear some of the risks of issuing them.

3.   Stock exchanges sell new issue stocks, but there is no market available for existing stocks and bonds that owners want to sell.

4.   A stock's real value, is its market value, the current price of a share in the stock market.

5.   Profits that are made from selling stock for more than it cost the investor is called dividends.

6. Common stocks are the among the riskiest of all securities.

7. Preferred stocks have a par value, a dividend promised and can be callable.

8. Any dividend payment missed on preferred stock due to financial hardship, need not be made up even if the financial situation improves.

9. There are more stringent rules to be listed on the New York Stock Exchange than that of the American Stock Exchange.

10. NASDAQ members are dealers who won the securities they buy and sell, at their own risk, consequently their is no trading floor.

MULTIPLE CHOICE QUESTIONS

1. According to the NY Stock Exchange, the number of Americans who own shares of stock in one for or another rose from 6 million in the early 1950s to well over:
   a. 50 million
   b. 60 million
   c. 70 million
   d. none of the above

2. Stocks and bonds are known as securities because they represent claims that are:
   a. secured
   b. asset-based
   c. SEC approved
   d. all of the above

3. Investment banks such as Merril Lynch provide important services such as:
   a. advise companies on timing
   b. bear some of the risks of issuing stocks
   c. create the distribution networks for moving new securities into the hands of investors.
   d. all of the above

4. The face value of a share of stock at the time it is originally issued is called the:
   a. market value
   b. book value
   c. par value
   d. none of above

5.   The riskiest of all securities are the:
               a. municipal bonds
               b. mutual funds
               c. common stocks
               d. all risks are the same

6.   Well established firms that provide investors secure income from consistent patters of
       dividend payouts are called:
               a. preferred stocks
               b. callable stocks
               c. blue chip stocks
               d. cumulative preferred stock

7.   In order to be listed on the NY Stock exchange a corporation must meet certain minimum
       requirements as to its:
               a. earning power
               b. total value of outstanding stock
               c. number of shareholders
               d. all of the above

8.   Bonds are rated by Moody's and Standard & Poor with the best rating being:
               a. Aaa
               b. AAA
               c. C
               d. D

9.   The bond that is not taxable is the:
               a. Municipal bond
               b. Treasury bond
               c. Government bonds
               d. All bonds are taxable

10.   Bonds that require bondholders to clip coupons from certificates and send them to the
       issuer in order to receive payment are called:
               a. registered bonds
               b. bearer bonds
               c. discount bonds
               d. secured bonds

11.   Bonds that are unsecured are called:
               a. debenture bonds
               b callable bonds
               c. serial bonds
               d. convertible bonds

12. A recent survey found that more investors fall into the attitude category:
   a. daring
   b. conservative
   c. apprehensive
   d. none of the above

13. Usually, buyers of futures contracts need not put up full purchase amounts, rather the buyer posts a smaller amount, that is called buying on:
   a. margin
   b. quotation
   c. consignment
   d. all of the above

14. Stock quotations of the day-before transactions can be found:
   a. only in the Wall Street Journal
   b. only in the New York Times
   c. in most newspapers
   d. only in financial newspapers

15. The index that is a broader reporter because its list consists of 500 stocks: 400 industrial firms, 40 utilities, and 20 transportation companies is the:
   a. Standard and Poor's Index
   b. Dow Jones Industrial Average Index
   c. the NASDAQ index
   d. all of the above

ANSWERS TO TRUE AND FALSE QUESTIONS

1. True	6. True
2. True	7. True
3. False	8. False
4. True	9. True
5. False	10. True

ANSWERS TO MULTIPLE CHOICE QUESTIONS

1. A	6. C	11. A
2. D	7. D	12. B
3. D	8. B	13. A
4. C	9. A	14. C
5. C	10. B	15. A